# The
# Freaks Shall
# Inherit the Earth

# The Freaks Shall Inherit the Earth

### Entrepreneurship for Weirdos, Misfits, and World Dominators

Chris Brogan

WILEY

*To Violette and Harold, who are the best freaks I know.
To anyone who's ever felt like the misfit or the weirdo:
you will inherit the earth (with some work).*

# Contents

# Preface

*The Guardians of the Galaxy* is being made into a movie.

As the first edition of this book goes to press (wishful thinking implied here), Marvel is releasing probably their weirdest and most risky movie idea to date. Made from a crazy comic book that covers a bunch of misfits engaged in intergalactic warfare, the cast involves a tattooed warrior, the daughter of a supervillain, a tree-like creature that says only one word repeatedly throughout the movie, and an alien that looks every bit like a raccoon, but don't let him hear you say that. Oh, and a "funny" human, so that we have a point-of-view character.

What does this have to do with business? Well, first off, movies are pretty big business, right? They cost millions to make, require hundreds of approvals, and expect to draw millions of people to the theater to see them. Who in their right mind thought *The Guardians of the Galaxy* would be a good movie for Marvel to put up on the screen?

The freaks already have inherited the earth, my friend. Weirdos and misfits are now the world dominators. It used to be that all the crazy fringe interests of the world were absolutely underground. Now, the underground has become the core of a thriving and somewhat hard-to-track new economy. Trends have a hard time covering this stuff, unless we start squinting.

That jobless recovery? Where are all those people going? I'll tell you one group of people who aren't rushing back to their cubicles: freaks. Instead, they're becoming artisan pickle makers in Brooklyn, punk rock dog groomers in Memphis, and zombie apocalypse race organizers in Boston. More experiences like this happen all the time.

Are you using your degree as it was intended in your current job? Lots of people aren't. How is the education system keeping up with the velocity of change in what actually constitutes a real job? There are thousands of people who can now list "YouTube celebrity" or "podcasting megastar" on their tax return, thereafter reporting their seven-figure experience for the previous year. You can't get a degree in making YouTube videos (yet).

Is this book for you? Man, I really hope so. I hope this book is a battle cry, a belief that "I can totally do this," and provides a sense of support, especially if you're not getting it elsewhere. Skateboarder and businessman Tony Hawk said his parents supported his choices from an early age, but that's not always the case. Some freaks have to buck a lot of family and friends to go where their heart says to go.

Well, here's your first opportunity to join that revolution yourself. Or at least to feel like you're not alone, which is a really powerful feeling if you ask me.

If you bought this book, thank you. If you took this out of the library, well, I grew up hiding in libraries and plotting world domination between the stacks. If you have in some way been forced to read this by a teacher or professor, I swear I never knew my books would be used for homework. If you get stuck, I promise I'll help (chris@ownermag.com).

If you're reading this in the hopes that it'll motivate you to buy the book, ask yourself a simple question: Are you someone who really wants to blend in and be part of the background, or do you secretly have a wild side, maybe a hidden tattoo, and are awaiting the battle cry?

Calling all freaks!

Oh, and you don't have to like *The Guardians of the Galaxy*. We're not all into the same stuff. That would be conformity. Right?

# 1 Business New and Old and New Again

**D**isruption has become the norm in business. But this doesn't always mean massive and world-changing disruption. Sometimes, it just means that the world is a bit more open to conducting business the way you'd prefer to do it these days.

I'm writing these lines in a hotel room, but I could just as easily be staying in someone else's guest room, thanks to AirBNB.

Earlier today, I had a call with a woman who heads marketing for a software company. She chose the job so she could work from home, spend more time running, and not have to spend time in a cubicle. I referred a purple-haired girl who used to work at a reputable Canadian company for a freelance gig in Dallas where the young woman will be working at the kind of company that wouldn't normally hire someone with purple hair. But these days, they will.

Why? Because the freaks are about to inherit the earth.

## Okay, What Does This Really Mean?

You picked up this book for one of a few reasons:

- You know me already and just want to see what I'm jabbering about this time.

- You want to know what a book about freaks is really about.
- You've felt like a freak (or like one that is in hiding) for much of your life and are wondering if I can offer any advice.

The premise of this book is really simple: How can I do business my way and be successful, when the way I think and the goals I have aren't in line with conventional thinking?

Does that resonate with you? Then you're in the right place. Not sure? Well, perhaps you should keep reading. If you love fitting in, doing what you're told, and being just like everybody else, you're going to have a bad time (http://hbway.com/badtime).

This book is designed to help you stop doing the things that aren't working for you, and start taking action with the things that will. It will enhance your confidence and understanding of who you really are, and help you determine how to develop an approach that works best for the people you intend to serve. That's one of the best thing about this book's message: In the old days, you had to conform. Now, you only need consider your choices and choose the options that feel most right to you.

## Am *I* a Freak? Are *You*?

Are you a freak? Are you a misfit? A world dominator? A small army? I'll let you know right off the bat that I am a freak. I've always had to do things my own way. I don't usually fit in, at least not without having to make a lot of effort. I don't choose the easy route. If there's a difficult way to get something done, I'll choose that way. Case in point: I wrote this entire book twice because I didn't like the way it came out the first time. From an early age, I felt that the world at large seemed like it was running on autopilot. And I wanted to take the wheel.

What's your story? Maybe you are the CEO of your own cubicle, or an *employeepreneur*, a title coined by my friend James Altucher—never quite satisfied to toe the line, but instead, working hard from your corporate role to make the company far more amazing. Maybe you're the 61-year-old grandmother who is a rock vixen at heart, who can't get over the fact that you have grandkids, and who still wears leopard-print pants to the business mixers.

Or maybe you're a business owner who has never really done business the way the rules dictate that you should. Maybe this has worked great for a while, but now you're feeling pressured to do things "the regular way" to get through tough times. Perish the thought, I say. Stay the freak that you are! We'll figure out how to get through together.

Let's agree to this: You can call yourself whatever you like, but you're a freak if:

- You don't fit in without some serious effort.
- You are not a big fan of settling or compromising.
- You're looking for ways to allow your weirdness to be an asset, and not as the deficit that people have tried to convince you it is.

## Is There Some Age Limit to Freaks?

People often wonder whether freaks are more frequently young people. But some of the most interesting freaks are older than you might imagine. Here's a story about one.

Many years ago, I worked in a nursing home. One of our residents was Helen. She was 104 years old. Her breakfast, every morning, was oatmeal with black licorice on top. I asked her about it one time. She said, "I can eat whatever I like at this age. Who will say a thing about it?"

Many older people tend to take a magical viewpoint as they age: They simply don't care if they don't fit in, Admittedly, this is a broad generalization, but it does beg the question: Why wait to be old to do what you want to? You can start deciding to be who you want to be— not caring what people think about it—whenever you choose. It's yours to explore.

# But What Does This Have to Do with Business?

For quite some time, there has been only one mainstream method of operating in the modern business world: fit in, or get out. The industrial era encouraged the notion that we needed consistency, that there had to be regular hours of operation, that people had to conform to very specific and measurable modes and decisions. If you weren't willing to follow these standards, you were an outcast and business wasn't going to happen.

So many things have changed in recent times. For one, new opportunities for employment have surfaced. Let's say you have always wanted to work for a car company—but not any of the established ones. Nowadays, you can work with Local Motors (localmotors.com), and simply design your own car. Maybe you've always wanted to design every single texture used in a room of your house. That's an option now, thanks to 3-D printing (hbway.com/3droom).

You want to create and sell your art? Great. Mobile payment company Square makes that easy (squareup.com). Need a place to meet that isn't a coffee shop or hotel lobby? Breather can find you exactly the right space (breather.com, which happens to be run by my sometimes coauthor and all-times friend, Julien Smith). You want to rent out your place in New York so that you can travel the globe? Make money by putting your apartment up for rent on AirBNB (airbnb.com).

Opportunity abounds where there were never any before. For instance, I'm a magazine junkie. I love to read them, and I've had the pleasure to write for several great ones. But then I launched my own because, why not? (ownermag.com).

That's just it. The challenge for the past 100 years or so was to find a job and *maybe* a career. Today, you can choose the work you want to do and find a way to do it the way that makes the most sense for you and your buyers.

Marie Forleo found this out for herself early in life: "I used to work on the floor of the New York Stock Exchange. That was my number-one job pick out of college and I loved it because there were no chairs. I had a lot of energy and I felt like, 'This is the only kind of environment where I can be as crazy as I am and I'm going to match with everybody else.' "

But Marie soon came to see that the fit wasn't *entirely* there.

"[When I was on] Wall Street, I realized, 'God, this isn't *it*—because my heart isn't in it.' I kept having this intuitive gut feeling, 'This is not where I'm supposed to be in life.' The scary part was, I didn't know *what else* I should be doing because all the other job descriptions I'd been exposed to at that point sounded boring as hell."

Marie went on to try out magazine publishing, starting out in ad sales and moving around a bit more. She then moved into the editorial side at *Mademoiselle* magazine, but it still didn't feel quite right. As she tells it:

I was on the Internet, probably when I shouldn't have been, and I stumbled across this article about a "new profession" at the time called life coaching. And I kid you not, something in me just [knew this was for me]. I was about 22 or 23 years old—and even though I knew it was ridiculous to think that anyone in their right mind would [hire me; after all], who would hire a 23-year-old life coach? I could not deny that something inside of my heart and my being was lighting up like nothing ever had lit up before.

So fast-forward a couple of months. I had signed up for a coach-training program. It was a pretty lengthy one, but I got a call from Condé Nast HR. They wanted to offer me a job at *Vogue*—the queen bee of fashion magazines. That was my fork in the road, [the moment] when I said to myself, "Okay, either you're going to take this job at *Vogue*, and continue on this kind of publishing career, or you're going to quit and start your own life-coaching business at 23." So, of course, you know what I decided to do. I quit, started bartending at night, and began building my coaching business during the day. That's really where it all came from.

Marie is still writing her success story. But she crossed the seven-figure line in earnings for her business a few years ago and there's no end in sight. Marie Forleo definitely qualifies as a freak inheriting the earth. Her quirky humor and style shines through in everything she does. Check her out at marieforleo.com, and also see http://hbway .com/marievideo for an example of her video stylings.

## You Don't Have to Wait for Permission

John Saddington loves creating useful software—and he loves it when an itch that he needs to scratch in his own life turns out to help others, as well. Such was the case when Saddington developed Pressgram (pressgr.am), an application and WordPress theme pairing that allows you to easily post photos from your smartphone to your website. If it sounds just a *little bit* like Instagram, that's because it is. Only you can create your own Instagram-like experience using Pressgram, and obviously have a lot more control over it.

Saddington was just launching the software when I interviewed him. I asked him how he went from being a guy with a day job to a guy running his own small business. He claimed it wasn't all that difficult; he launched a Kickstarter program and asked people whether they'd support his project. They funded him to the tune of about $56,000, which let John focus full-time on Pressgram. The people voted with their money, with no middleman in sight. That's how we will inherit the earth, my fellow freaks.

Saddington is already working on new projects and developing whatever else makes sense for the community he has built around himself. He does this from the empire of his own home, with his children happily running around him. The business could exist literally anywhere there's a decent Internet connection—like so many other businesses out there, including my own.

This book isn't about the Internet being the salvation of all companies out there. And even though you don't need to be some kind of online business to be a freak, I can say that the Internet is one of the tools that is helping to empower people to be who they want to be.

# Can You Be Sure of the Outcome Before You Start? Not a Chance!

R.J. Diaz runs Industry Portage (industryportage.com), a company that produces laptop bags, duffel bags, and other utilitarian goods with a kind of rugged beauty. R.J. comes from the construction industry, which isn't a field that's generally known for its fashion sense. I asked him whether his friends and business colleagues teased him when he first launched the company. He replied:

> I don't have a background in textiles or fashion design at all. They know that there's an artistic side to me, but I still got a strong reaction of, "Why would you ever do that? What do you know about making a product?" That reaction was tough to take. However, a lot of people were very supportive. Some members of the construction industry gave me sort of a smirk, like, "Okay, that's a nice hobby." They discounted me for awhile until I kept up with newsletters and new product designs. Soon they realized [it was time] to take me seriously.

I asked R.J. how hard it was to pull off this kind of project.

> If I [had known] then what I know now about having to develop this idea, I honestly don't know that I would [have done] it. [In the beginning], I talked to a bunch of different retailers, a lot of different material sources, both domestic and outside the U.S. [I wanted to find out] who would be willing to do small minimum quantities, who would be willing to work with me in terms of prototyping, sampling, and testing out products. That process took about a year. It was less than a year when I launched the website from the time I conceived of the Industry Portage brand and concept. I launched it on October 22—[which happens to be] my wedding anniversary and my daughter's birthday. I wanted to tie that all together with the hope that it becomes

something [of] a legacy that maybe my kids can carry. But for now, I'm still in building mode.

Diaz continues to work on building Industry Portage into a brand that makes sense for both construction and architectural workers, but also for people who appreciate style and rugged good looks. To look at him, you wouldn't think R.J. Diaz is much of a freak. He's fashionable, stylish, and quite successful both in his construction business and on the path to success with Industry Portage—which just goes to show that freaks aren't always easy to spot.

## Freaks Often Find Their Own Distribution Paths

You don't have to wait for permission to turn your entrepreneurial vision into a reality. However, you *do* have to find a way to get your product or service to the people who will want to purchase it. Hugh Howey didn't wait for permission when he published his Wool series of science fiction books, about life in a series of silos in a postapocalyptic world. He just wrote the books and published them on Amazon's Kindle Direct Publishing platform. After some fairly significant sales via his own efforts, publishing giant Simon & Schuster inked a deal with Howey for the print distribution rights to the book—which ended up being worth another $500,000 on top of what he'd already made on his own via digital distribution.

And just in case that wasn't interesting enough, Howey sold the rights to the movie version of the Wool series, showing us yet again that the mainstream doesn't have to be your only path into a success that matters to you.

## Challenges That Stand in Your Way

Of course, there are many ways you might find your path to success thwarted. You might find money getting tight and feel the urge to surrender your unique style and intentions and try to fit in. You might quit too soon.

Some other challenges you might face along the way:

- **Lack of a clear goal.** How will you know what success means to you if you don't define it? Make sure you have a clear and defined idea of your goal. It's okay if you don't end up there as long as you are moving in that general direction. I go into this in detail in Chapter 2 for the very reason that so few people have a goal in mind.
- **Seeking money from the wrong part of the value chain.** Looking for your money in the wrong part of the chain may thwart you early on. I meet a lot of people who want to build businesses to serve bands. But most bands don't have a lot of money. However, the *venues who book bands* make money from bands. The organizations that supply and equip bands with their gear have lots of money. Be sure you know both who you are serving and who your customer is.
- **Feeling of isolation.** Being different (a freak!) means often being surrounded by people who don't "get" you. There's a huge push to surrender, to conform, to think, "maybe I *am* wrong." But get a second opinion before you agree, and even a third opinion—and from freaks, not from "normals." You'll soon find that your gut feeling has been right all along—and that *being different* is what will keep you headed toward success.

## Business Is about Belonging

I've received compliments with a consistent theme over the past decade or so. People tell me, "You really do care about people," and "I feel like you see me and understand me," and "I've really enjoyed meeting and getting to know the people you've gathered into your community." I'm proud of this, of course—but only because it continues to confirm a business tenet in which I believe strongly. Though you'll rarely find it out there in the textbooks, if you listen and read closely, you'll find in the works of many successful people: Business is about *belonging*.

It might seem strange that a book that encourages freakiness and the refusal to fit in praises the idea of belonging. But you can see how these two ideas are different, correct? "Fitting in" often means shaving off your unique edges, hiding and masking what defines you, discarding any behaviors or appearances or images that prompt others to question you or push away from you. "Belonging" is about finding that place where you finally let out a deep breath you had no idea you were holding and feeling with great certainty that the people around you *understand you*.

Raul Colon is a friend of mine and a successful business consultant, as well as one of the Spanish-language writers inside the pages of my magazine, *Owner*. Raul is also a vegan, which means that he doesn't eat or use any animal products whatsoever. This is a challenge because Raul lives in Puerto Rico, where meat is a big part of the culture. He's told me many stories of friends and relatives saying to him that they are vegetarian, and then watching them eat pork. When questioned, they say, "Well, it's not beef."

Restaurants everywhere face a challenge when considering whether and *how* to serve the vegetarian and vegan (and other dietary choice) communities. Raul wrote a piece for *Owner* where he commented on the big difference between a restaurant that grudgingly ensures that a salad has no animal products, and one that proudly displays a wide selection of dishes specifically targeted for vegans. The difference, of course, is that when Raul finds a restaurant that welcomes his business, he spends more of his money there. He feels that he *belongs*.

Harley Davidson might be one of the brands that is most famous for creating a sense of community. People who wear suits and dresses during work hours keep their Harley keychains and "My Other Car Is a Harley" bumper stickers handy to remind themselves and others that *this is where they belong*. Some books have looked at this kind of branding as tribal. What we've come to co-opt as the concept of tribes is built on belonging, as well.

I started by telling you how business was new and old and new again; how this concept of belonging has been with us since before commerce. Yet we tend to create complexities that try to smother that sense of belonging, or we attempt to be all things to everyone. And all that does is to make us lose our powerful edge. When you make it your business to find the people who are the same *kind* of freak as you, you'll profit from serving that community in some form or fashion.

# 2 The Wild Colors and the Solid Spine

## What Makes Some Freaks Successful and Other Freaks Strugglers?

While plenty of the most unique people take pride in showing off their wild colors, many are lacking an important element in turning their freakiness into success. The one missing ingredient most would-be world-changing freaks lack is their ability to answer the question, "How is this a business?" In other words, what are these people offering that can truly make an impact . . . and a profit?

You know wild-color people. They marker up their sneakers. They paint their hair. They have notebooks full of great ideas. They most likely still have a day job (and that's okay). They love being artistic.

But the folks with the "solid spine" have learned how to be weird *and* run a business. I'm not sure exactly how people discover it for themselves, but what I've observed suggests that most people find it through the necessity—or very strong desire—to make money.

Author and speaker Chris Guillebeau would be an interesting fellow if all he did was fly around to different countries. But he's a business professional because he's come up with ways to help others with similar passions, and because he's developed products and projects that generate revenue while giving a lot back to the people he has the pleasure to serve.

When I ask people "What's your business?," I get some interesting answers back. Someone just told me (mere moments before I typed these words), "My business is to spread inspiration and joy." I think she has the word "business" confused with "mission." She might want to spread inspiration and joy—but is that something people will pay for?

Maybe so. After all, we are paying for inspiration when we buy T-shirts and mugs and posters with slogans on them. Heck, we buy running shoes because we like the ads. And yet, what counts is that last-mile challenge of knowing how to extract value for the spreading of inspiration and joy. *That's* the difficult part for most of the wonderful freaks I know.

## Those Pesky Coins

It takes a special individual to understand business yet retain a wild, creative mind. You have to understand how to create value that someone wants to pay for, yet try never to settle for something less than what you know to be what you want and can do and feel passionate about making happen.

First, there are some musts. You must be able to pay your bills. You must invoice people so they pay you (or collect money from them in some way). You must create something to sell (even if it's a service). Without that, you don't have a business; you are just being creative or you have a hobby. You can avoid doing a lot of things, but not these things. They *can* be handed off, if you want to spend some money and delegate these chores. Plenty of not-so-creative people are still entrepreneurial enough to partner with ultra-creative types, and they're more than happy to deal with the details that I and many other freaks might consider drudgeries.

Second, while you try never to settle, it's sometimes necessary to do so. Sometimes, you pay some bills. Sometimes you do what's "good enough" because you have to get moving to stay alive. There are lots of times when what you think of as ideal isn't where you end up in the execution.

So there are two sides to the coin: You must do what it takes to do business, but you must also stay true to your vision and not land in the realm of settling. That's the challenge, the paradox, the needle you have to thread to be able to make the solid spine make sense.

Of course, it can be a little simpler to do this if you think of your artistic work more as a craft instead of just an abstract object of art.

## Embedding Art into Your Craft

Some would say that we need art to live—a first-world perspective, for sure. But I will say that those things we need and want always turn out better and more beloved if we infuse a little art into them. To my mind, embedding a little art into your craft, whatever that may be, is the touch that allows one to show off his or her wild colors while keeping a solid foundation to his or her business.

Fashion designer Marc Ecko started by airbrushing clothing with graffiti designs and painting people's nails. He wanted some money to do what he wanted to do. His passions turned into a company worth hundreds of millions. He's never compromised the freak side of his wild colors, but all along, Marc has created products that speak to a certain community. Members of that culture seek out these products to show others that they belong.

No matter what your business is, you can incorporate creativity into your craft. Christopher Lynn, director of sales and marketing at Boston's Colonnade Hotel, has found a way to infuse creativity into his business. Ever attentive to his repeat guests, Christopher is quick to add an artistic touch to someone's hotel stay, such as tossing a Black Keys CD onto my bed while I was out at a concert. He once told me the story of how two brothers competed to inherit a liquor business from their father by creating and marketing their own beverage—while ordering me a cocktail made with that same product. Though I can't technically call Christopher Lynn a freak (he dresses too nicely), I can say that he has an artistic brand with a business bent—and that should be your goal as well.

## Know the Basics of Business

So how does this approach fit into the mechanics of a business?

A company's goal is to sell *something of value to a buyer*. It exists to offer a service or product in exchange for some kind of payment. Simple, right?

Business *models* are methods for making this exchange happen. For instance, there's a very basic model for media businesses like mine. For most businesses, this can be illustrated by a triangle:

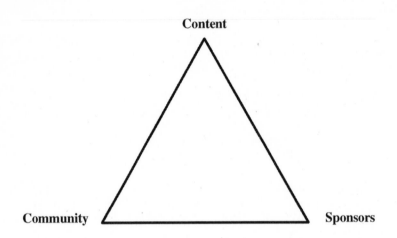

The top point in the triangle refers to the valuable content that helps and entertains. The bottom left point is the community that comes to read and experience that content. The bottom right point is the sponsor or advertiser who pays the content's producer for the opportunity to advertise to the community that has gathered to consume the content.

For example, if you own a magazine, your *customer* is the advertiser. You hope to cultivate readers, but you exist to improve the potential for advertisers to reach customers who engage with their ads. That's what makes the business work. Unless you're Oprah. Or Howard Stern. Or me.

Yes, we all have to do something to make money—and have some kind of relationship with an advertiser or sponsor or partner to make our media business viable. But the goal for my business is to attract the community of people who see themselves as important and valuable to me. I then concentrate on nurturing that relationship with them so that they trust that the kinds of people I choose to partner with and take on as advertisers are people *they* might also come to appreciate.

That's the freak's method of building a media business.

## Other Business Models

Lots of people have a product model: make something, sell it, repeat. Other people have a service model: know something that others don't know or don't care that they know, and do something for your buyer that he or she can't or doesn't want to do. Easy, right?

There are also all kinds of people with prestigious degrees and decades of management and leadership experience who will tell you about every 10 years that if you're in the product business, you should launch a service business. Then they'll tell you that if you have a service business, you need a product. Okay.

To me, the crucial question is: Are you seeking a *transactional* or a *relationship* experience with your buyers?

For most real estate professionals, the goal of their business is to get the most profit possible for their seller, or save the most money possible for their buyer—all while closing the deal on a house. There are really only three elements in this business model: the property, the seller, and the buyer.

That is, unless you're a freak. Then you see the real estate business as a chance to express your creative side and your artistic bent on building relationships. And if that's the case, your goal is to earn so many referrals and so much continued connectivity to your client that you will never worry about staying in business because you have developed a caring touch.

The Corcoran Group in New York City sells real estate, pretty high-end stuff. Instead of just showing how many rooms or how new the kitchen is, we are treated to stories that go beyond the walls. We learn a lot about the people who inhabit the houses, who breathe life into them. It's art. You don't have to do all this to sell a house, so why do they do that? It's the experience.

Let's say you sell hamburgers, and then decide that you want a transactional business. I have eaten many a hamburger from a place that wants me to simply pay and leave. But if you're Joe Sorge in Milwaukee, Wisconsin, you sell "fun with a side of burgers" at their AJ Bombers restaurants. Joe runs a relationship business that happens to sell burgers. And he has several other types of restaurants in town, so building a positive relationship means that when someone doesn't feel like burgers, they can have barbecue at his Smoke Shack. If they want salad for lunch, they can swing by the Water Buffalo. Joe's staff at each of these locations, no matter the food type, will treat you in a similar, positive way.

Is Joe a freak for caring? Probably. His barbecue joint, for instance, uses only the best-quality meat (grass-fed and free-range animals, for example). That's the opposite of the entire premise of barbecue: do things to the meat to make you not care that it's not the best-quality cut or product. But that's where Joe has incorporated the wild colors into his very solid spine. He'll take less of a margin on his food provided you come away feeling very positive about the experience and therefore likely to spend more with him over time.

There are plenty of business models out there. And while we won't focus *too* much on them in this book, I challenge you to do something right now. Take a moment and a piece of paper and write out what your business model really is; that is, try to remove all the buzzwords and just focus clearly on what you do and who buys it. See if what you've written makes sense to you. Hint: If your business seems more complex than it should be, you can do better. Simplify it more.

## Our Fear and How It Messes Up Our Businesses

I once asked an executive about to speak at an event what he did for Unilever. Without missing a beat, he said, "I sell soap." At that point in my career, I *really* cared what my business cards said. I had a terribly silly title that I thought made me seem really important, but probably just confused the people who saw it. This C-level individual's crystal-clear assessment of his role—"I sell soap"—made me realize how unnecessary all that extra wording was.

My old boss at the wireless company (technically my boss's boss, and eventually my boss's boss's boss) where I worked early in my career began a meeting with me and about 30 other people by asking us to do the "around the table introductions" dance. My direct boss at the time said her name and then used a title that had about 24 words in it, also explaining her context. When it came time for her boss to say what he did, he said, "Bill. Technology." And everyone in the room suddenly knew who had the power.

We tend to make things more complex when we fear that others won't take us seriously—or, when we worry that what we do seems silly or too easy. We also make things more confusing than they need to be when we want to give the impression that what we're doing is new.

And yet, we run into lots of experiences in life in which we learn that this isn't such a great idea. Ever head to the restrooms at a popular restaurant only to have to puzzle over whether you're a "squid" or a "shark?" "Roosters" and "hens" and the like seem clever. Just tell me where to pee, okay?

Complexity serves nothing but our ego. Be able to say what you do in a way that people can understand.

## Fear Is Probably Your Business's Worst "Competitor"

Lots of people tell me they're "bad at sales." When I ask them how often they actually *try to sell*, they usually answer by pointing their eyes at the floor and swaying in place. People are bad at selling because they don't practice it much. There are lots of ways that this manifests itself and lots of ways that we mask it.

I'm really bad at cold-calling. If someone doesn't know who I am already and hasn't started the conversation, I really don't know what to say in that weird business dance that others do. Maybe that's one reason why I started a media business. I can create posts and videos and audio and then you can comment, and if through that experience, I see that there's something I can offer you, I might be able to talk to you. See? It's sneaky, but it's clearly hiding the fact that I'm not good at introducing myself.

Most of what we fear is tied clearly to what we don't know. If we're not sure which steps to take, we balk at the process. If you don't know how to build up a list of people to call in order to pitch them something you're selling, you'll avoid even starting the process. We dodge those things that cause us discomfort as often as we can in life.

But the more we try something, the more we learn about what not to do and what works well enough for us. The more we practice, the more we'll understand when someone gives us tips or pointers. Without practice, how will we get to better understand what we don't do well, what we don't know, and where we can find our next opportunity to improve?

## Missing Ingredient: Discipline

I get certain questions more than others. Lots of people seem to want to know "How do you find the willpower to exercise (or write or whatever) every day?" It's interesting that people rush right to "willpower" as the answer to what I'm doing. Because I'll share a little secret with you: *Willpower is one of the smallest mental muscles you have.*

## Willpower Will Let You Down

When you're operating from willpower, you're saying "I really, really, really want this thing, but o-o-o-kay, I know. I'll be 'good.' " It's the unnatural order. In the Heath Brothers' parlance in *Switch*, it's a mad charging elephant rushing toward its goal, with you, the little rider clutching the reins, whispering a request to stop.

Willpower is a muscle. If it were on your arm, it would be one of those teeny tiny muscles hiding underneath the ones you want to show off at the beach. It's a supporting cast member, but it tires easily. You're looking for the big guns here: discipline.

## Discipline Is Where It's At

Willpower comes into play when you are working from a higher vision; you want to do something different and force yourself to do what you believe is the better/right choice. Discipline is what you call on when you've worked hard and built up a lot of repeat performance of the tasks you want to accomplish that you know are better/right, such that you intend to get it done and build your mental world around it.

Discipline is what keeps me from ordering a pastry at the coffee shop. I no longer even want them. I know that my body works better without eating them. I know that my goals don't seem to have "pastry" listed anywhere.

## How to Build Discipline

- **Change your program.** It starts in the language. If you claim to hate doing invoices, they'll never get easier to do. Instead, say "I love the grind. I love getting paid. I'm going to get this done so I can do other stuff I love, too."
- **Talk yourself into it.** Similar to the above concept, but with a little more execution. For instance, every night before I go to bed, I pop open the little notepad app that lists my gym workouts. I review what I'll be doing the next day. When I wake up, I tell myself that I'll go hit the gym before the day gets busy.
- **Start and keep a streak going.** Take out a calendar. Start doing one thing. Do it repeatedly for 60 or so days. *Just that one thing.* If some other things falter, it's okay. *Then*, add another thing after 60 days. Somewhere in the process, a *ton* of streaks will happen. This might sound silly but it's part of the process, and if you don't do it, you will likely not find discipline.
- **"Eat" lots of goodness.** No matter the discipline you're intending to install, fill your head with great examples and reinforcement. If you're working on getting fit, buy a bunch of fitness magazines. Follow inspiring leaders on social networks. Connect with awesome (we'll talk more about this later, but this is about discipline).
- **Carve away the badness.** If you're writing a book, TV isn't your friend. If you're working on losing weight, avoid the drive-through windows. There's no "both" in discipline. You are, or you are not. This is the hardest part. But if you whine about it, clearly you're in the "are not" category.

- **Work more than you celebrate.** The week after Julien Smith and I made the *New York Times* best-seller list, I went back to work writing and creating. When you win (in any sense of the word), the risk is that you will want to coast. Discipline is about the work, not the medals.

I don't want you to simply read this section, perhaps highlight the list, and then move on. I *want* you to:

- Print this. Write it down. Tear it out of the book. And *post it in a place where you'll see it.*
- Pick a goal to use to test this out.
- Do the work and make it work for you.

Will you? Oh, who knows? I can tell you that this is my seventh book, and that the ratio of people who say "I should do that" to the people who say "I tried that" is pretty dismal. Let's talk about this as it applies to your ability to build the solid spine you need to make a business out of your personal freakiness.

## "Should" Means "Won't"

Maybe you've noticed a slight change in my tone over the last handful of pages. I will admit to it. It's because there's a kind of "toughness" that's required to actually accomplish your goals and do something that's not the norm, and it requires you to take some action.

One of the major missing ingredients for people who decide that they want to be more entrepreneurial is simple action. There are lots of reasons why they are not taking steps toward success, and none of them are especially easy to hear.

- You might be lazy.
- You might think you have to wait for someone's permission.
- You may lack confidence.
- You may lack skill.
- You may lack resources.

Want to know a secret? I'll give you the answers to the above quiz.

- Stop being lazy. (Sorry. No other answer for this one.)
- You hereby have my permission. (No, really!)
- This takes work, but you can use the recipe that is given in the earlier section, "How to Build Discipline."
- Skills can be learned.
- Resources can be acquired.

## The "Experience" Lie

People tell me that they can't possibly do entrepreneurial things because they don't have experience. By the way, potential new bosses will also tell you that you don't have experience. Oh, the paradox. Experience is this thing that everyone says you need, until you get too much, and then the job is a little beneath you, or you're a little too "mature" to be cutting edge.

To get experience, *you need to do things—before* you know how to do them. I launched *Owner* magazine without any experience in running a magazine. I figured it couldn't be that much harder than writing my blog (it is), and that since I'd written for professional magazines, I'd figure it out. When I started a marketing consulting business, I had neither been a professional marketer nor had I ever run a consulting business. I would go into meetings with people who had degrees in marketing and all kinds of backgrounds, and I'd say "You know those things you do with those other things?" And they'd say all these official words back. I'd say, "Yeah, that. Well, what if we did *this* instead?" And sometimes they'd do it.

That's the trick. *Until someone else does something once, no one will think it can be done. Until someone else repeats it, everyone will think you're lucky. By the time everyone's doing it, who cares?*

But this isn't to suggest that you can't prepare and be ready for what comes next. In the next chapter, we go just a little bit deeper into what it takes to prepare to be the owner of your own destiny.

# 3 Choose Your Own Adventure: Defining Success

How one defines success says a lot about how one might come to achieve it. My personal definition of success is this: being able to say yes to what I want to do and say no to what I don't. I'm pretty fond of that definition. It lets me write books and spend time with my kids and my girlfriend. This is how I play, how I choose to spend the hours of my day, and, most important, how I do my business.

But that's my definition. If you haven't yet defined what success actually looks like to you, it's important to do that now. Most freaks I spoke to while writing this book each had their own very clear—and unique—take on success. And even more important, they were able to identify completely new paths to achieve it and were able to recognize easily how others were figuring this out, as well.

Straight out of college, Alexis Ohanian cofounded the very successful Reddit (reddit.com), sometimes called the "front page of the Internet." Ohanian has used that success to build the travel-pricing aggregation site Hipmunk, and a site that helps with causes and nonprofit efforts called Breadpig. When I spoke with him, Ohanian was promoting his book, *Without Their Permission*. We talked about how we don't need the gatekeepers of the past to be successful these days.

> One of the big reasons I'm so jealous of the generation [growing up now] is they are unencumbered by these same

biases. Some little girl in Des Moines can get up one morning and say, "You know what? I'm going to turn on my webcam and talk about what I want to do." And [while] a lot of it [might] be pretty inane and silly, one day she might start talking about something that she finds she's really passionate about; maybe it's My Little Pony. Maybe it's the crisis in Syria. I don't know. But she is going to build an audience who is going to grow up with her over time.

And as I mentioned in Chapter 1, Marie Forleo is someone who fits that description. Though she hasn't talked lately about My Little Pony, she's built a business that delivers value to her buyers, that lets her spread her message her way, and that delivers a feeling of connectedness. Coincidently, Marie also helps her community understand and create their own definition of success.

## What Does Success Look Like to You?

For people who feel like they're the odd person out, sometimes success isn't about a dollar amount as much as it's about feeling like you belong. For others, it's a matter of the ability to express one's creativity and uniqueness. And other times, success is just a matter of surviving in your own way.

If you don't define what success means to you, however, and understand the implications of what you choose, how will you know when you've reached your goal and are living the life you want? Let's look at what the elements of success are for you; maybe you can pick some of these ingredients for a recipe.

I like to tell people that success isn't a destination; it's a state. It's a little green light on your instrument panel that tells you, "Today, I'm feeling successful," as opposed to when it's flashing a red "No bueno today." This is one of two changes in mind-set that helps you be a really happy freak.

A lot of your nonfreak brethren don't have this knowledge. They think that success comes from working within the norm and maintaining the status quo, not rocking the boat. They love all that stuff that doesn't seem to work well for you.

With that in mind, let's talk about ingredients for your recipe.

# Ingredients for Your Own Personal Success Recipe

You won't need all of these ingredients; you can simply pick the ones that resonate most with you. That's what will help you find your way to success. Think of this as the cupboard where you store your baking supplies and spices and you're going to whip something up. Success cookies? Yes, please!

Here are the ingredients, in no particular order:

- **Money.** I might as well start with the one that's most on people's minds, because you do need money to live. Money buys food and pays for shelter, and most of us don't get these things for free. So, some level of money is required for your success. But how much? This is up to you to decide. The documentary film *Happy* stated repeatedly that there isn't a correlation between income and happiness. In fact, several people with very little material wealth ranked as the happiest people alive. I simply want enough to pay my bills and eat the occasional delicious meal, and maybe travel once or twice a year. Nothing fancy. You?

- **Time.** In my experience, this is often worth more than money. I can lose money and make it back, but if I lose time, I'm stuck. Each of us only gets a finite amount. Thus, I use time as a measure in considering my definition of success. Will this eat up too much time? Will I have to spend a lot of time doing something I don't want to do? Will I have to spend time doing something I dislike instead of spending it with the people I love? Could I do some of this at home? These are the questions that drive one of my own personal, most important metrics of success. It might or might not be the same for you.

- **Fame.** Some people won't feel successful until enough people know their name. They crave the spotlight. They want the adoration of millions. Lada Gaga said it: She lives for the applause. If fame's part of your equation, that'll take a little extra work; but don't ever feel guilty if that's part of what you want. Like most aspects of what we choose in life, fame is neither good nor bad: It's simply related to our choices. I'm a weird kind of "Internet famous." That is, I'm treated like a celebrity if I go to certain events, but 99.5 percent of the population has no idea who I am. I appreciate the mix.

- **Achievement.** This is the really interesting ingredient to the success recipe. Some people thrive on accomplishment and achievement. If they aren't number one in their category, haven't invented something, or haven't received a particularly important accolade, that's what they end up chasing in pursuit of their definition of success. Lots of people throw this into their personal success recipe, but they either have a deluded idea of what their goal might be, or it's too far out of reach. If they don't have an objective that is concrete enough, they end up chasing every potential expression of their dream. Achievement is a worthy pursuit, but you must be specific and clear on what you hope to accomplish.

- **Progress.** If you want the clever and excellent recipe ingredient to help you make success a part of your daily life, become a collector of progress. This is the younger sister to achievement, and way more fun to know—because achievement comes with a lot more expectations, a lot more chances to miss a mark, a lot more opportunities to cling to the past. But progress is active. You can visit it daily. It's a powerful part of a success recipe.

- **Health.** This is the ingredient that most of us forget to add to our definition of success: physical, mental, spiritual, and emotional/relationship health. If you're not working on all of these, your success may be short-lived—or it may come at the sacrifice of other elements of your whole self.

- **Serenity.** I don't know that peace is the best ingredient for success, since you usually have to sacrifice it repeatedly in the process of striving. But I think that serenity, as described in a famous prayer by the same name, strikes the right note, especially about accepting those things you cannot change.

* **Add your own ingredient.** You're a freak. You're defining this yourself. I'm sure I left out something you really want in your definition of success. *You* add it.

*I want people to think that I am smart.*

And then maybe share your recipe with me. Yes, I mean with me specifically. If you're willing and if you want, send an e-mail to chris@hbway.com with "My recipe for success" as the subject line. I'll respond. Who knows? Maybe it'll be the start of a great new friendship!

## Failure Is Most Definitely an Option

I know why people like to say "failure is not an option." But when they're saying that, they mean "surrender" or "settling" is not an option. Because you can—and even should–most *certainly* fail.

One of the best pieces of advice I ever received about failure comes from life coach and self-help guru Anthony Robbins. He said, "Instead of thinking of it as 'failure,' think of it as an outcome you didn't expect or want." This is huge. Take a moment. Read that out loud to yourself. You didn't get the raise you wanted? Was that a failure or was that an outcome you didn't want? Your client can't pay you in a timely fashion, so you've got to ask your parents for yet another loan? Is that a failure? Not if you look at it with a different mind-set.

To me, failure is definitely an option. You can fail plenty. In fact, nearly everything I do starts with a failure, a stumble, and then some learning. Then, I go into the phase of making it all work, and finding success. At least, most times I find success; sometimes I quit.

## Quitting Is an Option, Too

We've got some strange ideas about quitting. We see it as a sign of weakness, of defeat, of failure. No way. Quitting is awesome. Quitting is the way to build strength and greatness. If you're worried that I'm being sarcastic and it's not coming through, I'm not. I mean it. Sometimes, quitting is the coolest and most intelligent thing you can do.

I used to think I wanted to be an artist (pen-and-ink cartoons). But that doesn't pay the bills for many people. So now I can draw little cartoons while presenting to thousands of people on a stage. I used to think I wanted to be in a rock band, but that's a very long-shot business for a lot of people. So now I play guitar and all kinds of instruments with my girlfriend, Jacqueline Carly, and sometimes I play music during my professional events.

I quit a lot of things. I quit eating too many starchy things. I quit sitting on my butt all day and took up fitness and health. I quit thinking that staying up all night was cool; now, I sleep as many as 10 hours a day. I quit a lot of really bad relationship choices and other decisions that were destroying me from the inside. And I attempt and then quit business ideas like leaves falling off a tree.

Someone was really kind to me when they said, "I've seen you launch and quit more businesses in the span of a year than most people will ever quit in their lives." They meant it as a compliment, too. Because they knew that all my quitting was getting me closer to winning. Success came after learning what to do, what not to do, and how many aspects of life I can quit.

### A List of Things to Quit (If You Want)

- **Television** (and random web surfing). I gain hours of time each day that lots of people don't have because of this.
- **"Keeping up."** It's vastly overrated. I keep up with the people I love and the people I serve. I don't need to know what color options are newly available for the iPhone.
- **Following everyone who follows you online.** At first, it seemed like the polite thing to do, but it just adds noise and isn't really related to human friendship. It's okay. Follow who you want to follow.

*[handwritten margin note: There are different kinds - some people are just not worth keeping up with!]*

*People think we need Fred, B. I say no.*

- **Living up to others' expectations**. This is a huge one. Your parents wanted you to be a lawyer. Your classmates thought you'd be CEO of a huge corporation. Whoever else outside of your skull has been influencing your own choices? Quit. Fast. Often. Untangle from all that.
- **Meetings**. I have rules about meetings. Less than 20 minutes unless you pay me a heck of a lot to sit there. Ten minutes if I can manage it, which is not too often. Sometimes, but rarely, an e-mail can fix it.
- **Bragging**. It takes a lot of energy that's better spent elsewhere.
- **Gossip**. Ditto. Plus it bites your butt. *I so need to not do this.*
- **Hoping the world will like you**. I know—much easier said than. But the magic that opens up once you get past that worry is worth it in ways that you wouldn't believe. *Again - Wanting approval from Fred. B.*
- **Doing stuff out of a sense of obligation**. This one's tricky. You should pare down your obligations and also your sense of who you owe an obligation to in the first place.
- **Buying dumb things**. We are owned by the things we own.
  *Getting rid of stuff is freeing !!*

What else would you add to this list of what to quit? I bet you have lots more. Quit all over the damned place. It'll change your universe.

## Success Comes to You from Weird Places Sometimes

I wanted to be an author from the time I was five years old. Back then, I thought I would write comic books. (Still want to do that, by the way. Call me, Marvel or DC!) I spent the first 20 or so years of my life after the age of five telling everyone that I was an author. When I got a little older, I read books about writing. I bought magazines about writing. I bought books that showed me where I could submit my writing. I just kind of forgot one thing: *to actually write*.

When I started my first blog in 1998, Internet essays were called journals. I did it to publish my fiction because no one wanted to publish it. In all fairness to the magazines where I submitted my work,

I didn't do a great job of matching my writing to their requirements. It wasn't their fault. It was mine.

I wrote almost every day on my blog for years. And then one day, I realized I had actually been doing the work of being an author rather than just talking about it. Not too long after that, I was offered my first book deal by Wiley (who published this book, too).

It went down so oddly. By the time I was offered the deal, I was a little bit flip about it. Ellen Gerstein, who was running marketing for Wiley Business approached me at a conference, then peered sidelong at me and asked me why I hadn't written a book. And I answered that books take time and effort and so on, and that I was blogging daily and finding it greatly rewarding. Thank goodness I finally said yes to the deal.

But along the way, I realized that my goals and my success had come to me by a totally weird and circuitous route. Julien Smith and I made the *New York Times* best-seller list with that first book. Not bad for a first try, right?

But if I'd kept it in my head that I was going to be a very specific type of author, I probably wouldn't have much to show for that goal, even now, almost 40 years later (shudder). So keep an open mind about what you want, what is possible, and which path to take to get there. Opportunities may arise where you least expect them, and the path may be different from the one you charted, but the outcome might be better than you ever expected.

## That Mix of Wild Success and Finding Other Successes

It's important to develop a broad and wide-ranging view of what success might mean to you. My friend Rachel Gawell is an amazing cello player, and she has played with orchestras and bluegrass bands and a lot of other groups. As I have told her, being in a band is a fate I wouldn't wish on my worst enemy. You don't make a lot of money.

However, I also let her know that there's money in video games. And in corporate performances. And in partnering with people for projects that aren't your typical band or orchestra. That's the challenge: Can you find success in some other format than what you originally wanted?

I'm not saying to give up on your dreams (not even a little bit). I'm saying that if you make your dreams a lot more flexible, maybe you'll find more than one bite of success along the way.

## Success Rarely Just Happens

A long while back, I shot a video about what it takes to become an overnight success (http://hbway.com/overnight). The answer, as you probably already know, is that it takes years and years of hard work. But it takes more than that.

- *Success comes to those who make it easy for success to reach them.* Do you have an accessible website where people can find you and have you made it easy for people to contact you?
- *Success comes to those who help others far more often than they ask for help themselves.* People who lend a hand to others get a lot more out of life than those who show up with their hand out.
- *Success is a daily practice.* People ask me how I can write 4,000 words a day (comes in handy when writing a book like this one). It's daily practice. Everything that leads to success comes from daily practice. Your three-mile run. Your painting. Whatever you need to develop.

## Be Ready for Success

Success also favors the prepared. Similar to the prior point, it's good to think through the baseline for being ready to have a chance at success. One really important point that I intend to drill in repeatedly throughout this book is that it's never a great plan to "just quit my job and figure it out later."

One way that you can define your success is by having the breathing room to actually make a move and take an action. For instance, people have said to me, "Oh, I'd love to try my idea of opening a restaurant, but I have two kids and a mortgage." That's not a reason not to try. It's a reason to be prepared.

- If you've never done this, figure out exactly how much money you need to make to cover all of life's expenses each month. If you're an employee, whatever that number is, multiply it by 1.3 to cover tax withholdings and health care coverage and other related items.
- Have three months (minimum) set aside. It's okay if you aren't ready to do that yet, but make it one of the first and most important efforts of your business planning.
- Reassess where you spend your money. Are there credit cards you can pay off and stop using? Is there a car payment that you need to deal with? Decide what has to happen financially to give you a better shot at having the room you need for success—because it rarely comes right away.
- Are there small bites you can take that will let you test-run what you intend to do to make that success happen? Superstar freak Alexandra Franzen wrote a great post about how one might learn more about their big dream by starting with one room (http://hbway.com/oneroom).
- Don't have a plan B, but have a plan A that really makes a lot of sense, and that has more than one avenue of approach. I'm not in favor of having fallbacks. If you make your move and nothing happens, can you make a different move from a different angle and still try to make it work?
- Realize that success comes from doing more than everyone else. You can't be lazy *and* successful. It just doesn't work out—at least not for long.

I can state for certain that success is built on skills. In the next chapter, I dig into some of the skills you might need to accomplish your goals and inherit the earth. Some of these won't apply to where you are at this very moment, but because I cover a spectrum of skills, you'll be able to find yourself and know where to start digging in.

Good? Good. Let's go.

# 4 Skill Building for Your Business Goals

There are certain skills that are necessary to understanding and adapting ourselves to make our business (and ourselves) successful. Some of these ideas might not apply to your immediate needs. If so, this chapter might be one you come back to later.

You might be the CEO of your cubicle or an employeepreneur. You may be starting out on your own in a solo business. Or maybe you have a few employees. Or perhaps you already own a business but still feel there's a lot to learn before your unique style fits the needs of the business.

You can adapt this chapter's ideas to fit your role. If I mention a skill that might be better suited for someone still working for a corporation, but you have two employees in your own business, then adapt it. If you're not sure how, drop me a line: chris@ownermag.com. We'll work on it together.

## The Real Basics

This book is about entrepreneurship. It's not as much a basic how-to book as a "you can find a way to thrive, even if you're not the typical businessperson" kind of book. But there are some basics we should at least mention as skills you need to develop if you're going to inherit the earth. I'll also use this part to discuss some skills and knowledge you *don't* have to learn.

- **Basic legal contract skills.** Depending on what you're doing, a lot of what you'll have to know in business will involve a legal contract. Paying a lawyer is a great option, but learning about contracts and other simple legal matters will be really useful to your future. If you just cringed and recoiled a bit, that's okay. You'll be better off in the long run.
- **Basic finance skills.** Business is about exchanging money for value. No matter how you want to slice it, if you're trying to build a business and not just have a hobby, money is and will always be part of it. Not knowing about money doesn't make you noble; it makes you waste money, which eats up more time. Just the basics will help.
- **Simple marketing concepts.** Marketing is about understanding the marketplace that your products and/or service actually serve. If you make peacock-feather hats, or rebuild My Little Pony dolls into new versions, there's a marketplace of people interested in that work, and some who might buy it. Learn the simplest of ideas, and grow from there.
- **Sales skills.** Sales is one of those challenging areas lots of people feel they're bad at. But as I've already stated—they've truly just never learned, or don't practice it much. If you are planning your own path, even if it's to be an employeepreneur, you must learn more about sales. (In that case, "selling" might be simply selling your ideas to the boss, but that's still similar).

These are the basics. There are plenty of books to look into and websites to follow and courses you could take to help you acquire this skill. But it's kind of a must that you learn and continue learning about these four areas. I'll tell you that, based on my experience, every time my business has hit a wall somewhere, it's because I wasn't as good as I could be on the four basics. Sometimes, I don't know enough about marketing. Other times, my lack of experience with legal matters causes me to spend too much time and money paying someone else to educate me. It's probably one of the most difficult challenges of figuring out how to own more of your life: accepting that you have to learn a few skills you don't understand and maybe don't *really* want to know. I've yet to meet a street artist who wants to better understand finance, even if they want more money in their pockets.

The rest of these skills are a bit less traditional in nature, although they also have roots in very timeless truths. You'll find that a lot of what I preach comes off as common sense; yet what's most magical about it is that so few people practice these skills. So that's where you can thrive. You don't necessarily have to work on everything that comes next, but an awareness of what I feel might help you inherit the earth would be useful. Ready?

# Business Is about Belonging

A while ago, my friend and former boss, Jeff Pulver, told me something very important. He said that no matter how much money someone has or doesn't have, the one feeling that a lot of people really want to experience is that sense of being "on the inside." I know that I feel pretty special when the server at my favorite restaurant remembers what my preferred order is. When I go to buy clothing and the staff treats me like a very important guest, it's powerful.

I said it in Chapter 1, but it's important enough that I'll say it again here: Business is about belonging.

## Our Quasi-Tribal Nature

Along with tens of millions of other people, my kids and I love the video game Minecraft. I went to the movies wearing a pin that only someone who played the game would recognize (http://hbway.com/pin), and sure enough, the girl who took my drink and popcorn order said, "Hey, nice pin! I love Minecraft. I play it all the time."

We seek to identify with people *like us* all the time. If you're the pink-streak-in-your-hair kind or the bold-and-visible tattoo kind, you tend to make a little bit of eye contact with others who have made those choices, correct?

It's a great opportunity to find a bridge. My daughter just started at a new school. A boy there saw her drawing a My Little Pony character in her notebook and said, "Hey! I'm a Brony!" (This is what the male fans of My Little Pony call themselves: http://hbway.com/bronies). Instant connections happened, if only temporarily.

This all boils down to a really important part of freak-minded business: If you're going to be weird and "out there" but you want to run a successful business, you need a way to signal your "tribe" that they belong, that you have something for them—that you *understand them*.

*Who are the Bellevue Mine tribe? Who belongs?*

### Let Them Share the Identity

*How can I let them know they belong?*

*Adventure + Bucket List*

When I launched *Owner* magazine, I was very deliberate about the name. I wanted to attract people who were ownership-minded, not employees-waiting-for-life-to-be-served-to-them. I wanted a term that was a noun. You can *be* an owner. If I called it *Ownership*, that title doesn't draw people. I wanted people to say, "Oh, hey! That describes *me*! *I'm* an owner!" And so far, that has worked.

Sometimes you attract customers by how you describe what you offer. When Steve Jobs debuted the iPod, he said, "You can fit 1,000 songs in your pocket." He didn't say "We created something because we're so amazing." You, not me. Us, not you. See it?

So—how are you selling whatever you're doing?

One of the best ways to build your business, especially if it's based on how unique you are, is to remember the people whom you serve. Everything from knowing that Prabha prefers text messages to e-mails when you're notifying her of a delivery time for her order, to remembering that Anthony's birthday is October 6, so you should do something to send good wishes.

The compliment I've received repeatedly from people over the years has been for an act that is actually *very simple* but nearly miraculous in its effect. I *remember people*. I remember their names. I remember little bits of information from our last interaction. Some of what I remember may be details that I've written down, at least once. Other bits are just something I'm somehow trained to recall.

## A Little More about Name Magic

People love it when you say their name. It's one of the only sounds we can pick out of a crowd. It's powerful to us. Use someone's name and they will feel that slight bit *more* of a sense of belonging.

We meet a lot of people. Some of us (understandably) have a hard time remembering names. Here's how to get better at it.

- Upon meeting someone, make eye contact while shaking his or her hand and say his or her name back to them. "Hello, Sanjay."
- Within 30 seconds, say his or her name again. "Thanks, Sanjay, I'm lucky that way."
- As often as possible in the next 10 days or so, relate information about your meeting with that person and use his or her name, even if you're just rehearsing out loud to yourself. "Yesterday, I visited Sanjay and learned about his great new company."

If you miss someone's name and now feel awkward about asking for it again:

- Say, "I'm really sorry. I'm blanking on your name. Please remind me?"
- Repeat the above steps for meeting someone the first time.
- Don't feel weird. Lots of people have trouble remembering names. It's not just you.

If you're ever in a situation where you probably should remember someone's name and you'd be horribly embarrassed to ask for his or her name again (it happens, I know):

- Bring a friend.
- Introduce that friend to the person. "Have you met Kelly?"

- The person then says, "Hi, Kelly, I'm Sanjay."
- You are a stealth name ninja. (Unless they use the same trick.)

At a conference:

- Say the person's name without ever overtly looking at their badge.
- If you can't remember their name, get really good at reading a name badge from far away and then pretending not to look.

It's just a matter of making people feel that they matter. Give them every chance to feel important and they will remember that feeling. As famed poet Maya Angelou said, *"I've learned that people will forget what you said, people will forget what you did, but people will never forget how you made them feel."*

## See the Territory, Not the Map

Once during an interview, I was asked what it was like to have launched so many successful projects. I answered, "It's great that I've had so many chances to fail and learn. I'm lucky to not be hampered by the fear of not having the first clue what to do, and not knowing any better most of the time."

The answer clearly surprised my interviewer, but it's also the truth. All of my success comes from being willing to learn more than I already believe that I know. In fact, it's also a way to be strong in competing. If others are hampered by their knowledge, they're doomed to follow the map instead of seeing the territory that the map explains.

Jay-Z is a great example of this. It's a little strange calling him a hip-hop artist. It'd be like calling Richard Branson a magazine publisher. Both men have vision that goes beyond what everyone else is considering. The *Made in America* concept, for instance, is so much more than a single title conveys. For example, Jay took the idea of his own musical tour and blew it up into the concept of a movement celebrating diversity of music, culture, and the expression of acceptance.

As a result, he found a great sponsorship deal—a great raft of content that included not only big acts but also up-and-coming musicians. He has a very robust vending experience that celebrates small business owners, local business, and more.

Look at the elements of this in the abstract:

- Big name draws people to an event.
- Big name turns the event into a celebration of acceptance, making it a way to gather the freaks around you (remember: Business is about belonging).
- Experience supports and encourages independent owners and local owners, and yet nets a huge sponsor.
- Profit ensues.

While other rappers are talking about their great cars, Jay-Z is building a portfolio of products that span far beyond his own microphone. How? Because he never once looked at the map everyone else was using to view the territory. He looked directly at the landscape and found his way into the bigger games.

## Hone Your Understanding with Questions

I needed some advice recently, so I called my friend, James Altucher. He laughed and said, "It's funny, because this is something I already discussed earlier today. It's almost the same advice."

One of the biggest mistakes freaks and owners make when starting out is believing that they should have all the answers, and that asking questions is an admission of weakness. This couldn't be any further from the truth. Asking a smart question often saves you a lot of time, provided you're willing to run with the answer.

The challenge is to know *when* to ask questions, *which* questions to ask, and to be brave enough to ask the right questions to the right people. You've heard the expression "garbage in, garbage out." This is supremely true with question asking. Let's go through a few questions that are "garbage" and a few that are "gold" so that you get a better sense of what you might ask someone in pursuit of understanding and growing your business.

## Garbage and Gold Questions

Garbage question: "How can I make a million dollars?"

Gold question: "Where did you waste your time or make the biggest mistakes when you were starting out?"

Garbage question: "Who can you introduce me to that will help me grow?"

Gold question: "Who could I most help with what I'm working on right now?"

Garbage question: "How can you help me grow my business?"

Gold question: "What can I do to help you with your business?"

Garbage question: "What's the secret to your success?"

Gold question: "If you were to recommend one area of growth for me based on what you've seen, what would you recommend?"

Garbage question: "How should I price my offerings?"

Gold question: "What were some of the testing methods you used to determine what worked and what didn't for you?"

There are even better questions to ask, but that would require me knowing more about you and your goals. These are a bit generic simply to make the point. The best questions are not only more targeted, but they are posed to the people most suited to provide you with the best answers. For instance, I asked James questions about business deals because I think of him as one of the best business negotiators I know. If I wanted advice on color schemes, I would ask Josh Fisher, my friend and design collaborator.

We'll cover the importance of asking the right questions in Chapter 5. Let's move on to more skills you might master on the way to success.

# Sketch Simple Business Models

Even if you're gladly warming a desk within a corporation, it would behoove you to understand how various business models work. Some of the best educational material out there on this is a book, website, courses, and events, all under the name of *Business Model Generation* (www.businessmodelgeneration.com/). The book is great. The new tools are excellent ways to extend your understanding.

But if you want to work on identifying or establishing new business models for your own business, get out a notebook and identify business models around you. What's the actual model behind movie theaters? Is the $10 (or much more) ticket the money maker? No; it's the concessions. And the model to pay even closer attention to is the margin game. If it costs 8 cents to make the popcorn but you're paying $8 for a bucket of it, that's a pretty decent profit, right? So, the *real* goal of the movie theater business, and the magical metric, is "dollar per guest." (Or rupee per guest—you adjust this for me, okay?)

# What Comprises a Successful Business Model?

This is a great question. I'm glad I asked it for you.

## Elements of a Business Model

Here are the elements of a business model, all simple to follow.

- How do we make money?
- Who is our buyer?
- How do we produce what we sell?
- How do we distribute what we sell?
- Is there any "magical metric" that helps us boil down our measurements?

That's a somewhat ridiculously simplified list of the elements of a business model, but there they are.

So let's take my friend and coauthor Julien Smith's company, Breather (http://breather.com), as an example. This site provides a place to rent space for a short time (such as the duration of a meeting, or a nap, or a meditation session). The person with the space is the seller; the person who needs the space is the buyer. The broker of this transaction is Breather. So let's apply the questions we listed above to this example:

- **How does it make money?** The transaction fee on each booking.
- **Who is the buyer?** We have two buyers: people with space and people needing space.
- **How do you produce what you sell?** We have standards for what kinds of spaces can be let for Breather, plus we make a transactional app and related tools.
- **How do you distribute what you sell?** Not entirely applicable here, as the space is distributed already.
- **Is there a "magical metric?"** Transactions per day (or week or month)—I would suspect so, though I didn't ask Julien if this is the case.

Do this all the time. Get into the habit of thinking out business models. See if any of them help you better understand your own model or reveal new opportunities.

My own business, for instance, went through some shifts:

- **Model 1.** Launch a consulting/marketing agency.
- **Model 2.** Sell speeches and private consulting.
- **Model 3.** Sell courses.
- **Model 4.** Sell lead nurturing products (via *Owner* magazine).

In all of these cases, all the other details shifted, the metrics shifted, how many customers I needed shifted, and more. See how this can provide a better understanding of the various business models available to you?

The number-one mistake I see most fledgling freaks make is that their business model is flawed. This happens quite often:

misunderstanding who is the best possible buyer and setting up a business around a buying segment that isn't interested or able to buy your product or service.

One woman told me she wanted to launch a business to help nurses become better at giving care. I asked her, "Do you think the nurses believe they're giving poor care?" Silence. "Do you think they will be paid more if they give better care?" More silence. It might be a good wish or an idea that would help others—but sometimes, it's just not a business.

Practice understanding and thinking about and considering and toying with business models. Innovation abounds here. Jeff Bezos initially built Amazon to deliver books. But he was already thinking of what *else* he could deliver. He took on market after market. Then, he went into digital markets. At this point, if you really had to describe Amazon, it's a retailer of *everything*, more or less.

This brings up a point: whether or not you love a business doesn't mean you can't love its business model. People seem to like to complain about Walmart, but it is a powerful distribution platform and a masterful use of data to understand buyer wants and behaviors. I think about a few things when it comes to Walmart and business models:

- I would have to build an amazing product if I wanted to compete head-on with this retail giant.
- Distribution is a very important part of most business models (Walmart and Amazon tackle this in similar but different ways).
- If Walmart has the "lowest prices" end covered, it means I could choose to service the premium price end with a product or service.
- Data can be amazingly powerful, if you actually use it.

There are entire books written about that one company. This brief mention is simply an example of how you can identify business models all around you and understand how to innovate around them.

But who has time for all this kind of thinking? I'm glad you asked. I don't have time for it—and neither do you.

## Master Time

Let me be clear: You will *not* inherit the earth, nor you will be successful at most anything, if you can't figure out and master time. Not manage it. Managing is something miserable that people do when mastery isn't possible. Master it. Own it. Make time your big brother. You can do it.

There are a few secrets that people who get a lot done hold in common. These guidelines are so unremarkable that I almost don't want to share them. However, here's why I get a lot done and you don't. Some I've shared already, but they bear repeating here.

**What Not to Do**

- I don't watch TV.
- I don't try to keep up with anything particular online.
- I don't pay attention to much in the way of news. If Godzilla is knocking down my house, I'll hear about it.
- I try not to stay angry.
- I work on "now" and "soon" much more than I work on "eventually" or "in the past."
- I don't make other people's priorities mine, unless they are.

**What to Do**

1. I always have a plan.
2. I work that plan.
3. When exceptions come up, I try desperately to hold onto number 2.
4. I say no. Often.
5. I decide. Fast. Indecision is a time killer.

Here's one truth: You give up your time because sometimes it feels like there's an abundance of it—and our mental version of nature abhors a vacuum. So, if you find you've got extra time, maybe you start volunteering. This isn't necessarily a bad idea, of course; but we can all agree that too much of anything is a mess.

Maybe the volunteering ends up chewing up 10 or more hours a week. Then 20 hours. And then the boss assigns you to a new project, or you're the boss and your number-one supplier quits. Something atypical happens. And then it's too much. You're swamped. Sound familiar?

There's so much required to mastering time; for instance, I went back and added "5" to the "What to Do" list. _Decide_. People chew up tons of time in between options. In countless circumstances, deciding *something* is way more productive than holding off for one reason or another. Take a guess. It's better than wasting time.

Some people just suffered a huge belly clenching doubt at this point. "You can't just rush in!" But it's totally untrue. You *can* just rush in. And sometimes, you'll decide wrong. You'll mess it up. So you fix it. You move forward. In fact, I'm going to say I disagree with the song. Only fools *wait around*. You? Rush in. Do it!

Here are other ways to master time:

- Get an egg timer—a real-life egg timer. (http://hbway.com/eggtimer).
- Refuse meetings as often as possible. Try to handle as much business as possible via e-mail or via GoToMeeting, or perhaps by phone.
- If you must have meetings, set tight time frames. Ten to twenty minutes is plenty for most meetings (except brainstorming sessions).
- Refuse phone calls or any real-time interactions as often as possible (unless they are with your most important advisors, your best buyers, etc.)
- Have a plan. It's amazing how much time we waste when we don't have a neat and tidy list of the items that matter most to us.
- Put items that *matter most* on that plan. Wow, people often fill their to-do lists with silly tasks.
- Delegate. Outsource. Make tasks *not yours*. It's amazing. I pay a really wonderful woman (hi, Monique!) to wash, dry, and fold my laundry.

- Every week she gives me a few hours of time I can use to make magic. The world is full of opportunities for you to pay a little to earn a lot (of time). Find them.
- Build systems. Rob Hatch has a great course about this (http://hbway.com/psyw). We learned a lot about the benefit of building systems on our use of time, and we learn more about it daily.

On my way to building my own success in my own way—in becoming the freak that I am—a lot of truths and experiences have come to me. Some might work for you; others might not.

- Talking about how busy you are is like talking about your dietary choices. It's *technically* interesting, but more so to you than anyone else.
- When people tell you they're busy all the time, they are either very busy because they've not quite learned to master time, or they're not at all busy, but feel embarrassed about this fact. I *love* telling people I'm not busy. They often think I'm joking. I often am not.
- People can have a weird infatuation with not sleeping. Entrepreneurs love to brag about not sleeping. I love to sleep. I sleep 8 to 10 hours a night, almost every night. Sleep is great. It rebuilds your systems internally. It helps with weight loss. It's a great way to power your brain up for the next day's optimal thinking. (Hint: I've never seen a mythical brilliant breakthrough occur to someone who's miserable and overtired.)
- Whenever I don't have time, it's because of a choice I've made. Most times, those choices fall into two categories: I didn't have a plan so I didn't work the plan, or I said yes when I should have said no. The more I fix those two failings of mine, the more time I inherit. (For example, I handed in this book a few weeks later than I should have because I wasn't sticking to my plan.)
- When people ask you how you find the time to do all the work that you do, they really aren't asking you to answer that question. They're saying, "I haven't really managed to master time myself, and

I'm a bit envious and appreciative of your output." Shrug and smile politely and give a casual, vague answer. Explaining your personal time mastery methods wastes more time and the other person is almost never asking with the intent of learning this skill from you.

- The most time I ever got back from all my efforts came from learning how to untangle my mind through meditation. Wait— don't run away! I don't mean *fancy* meditation. I mean breathing in and out and simply stopping active thoughts about something that wasn't helpful. If someone is mad at you, and you spend hours and hours over a bunch of days thinking about that (and feeling bad or mad or powerless about it), think of how much time that really takes up. It's okay to feel bad, especially if you did something that brought about a negative experience for someone else. But remember this: Dwelling on the past and worrying about the future are a tax on the hours you have left on this planet. Why pay more taxes than necessary?

When you get down to it, time is one of those matters where we spend a lot of energy thinking about it, but managing it is quite simple. Each day has 24 hours. Plan your hours. Use your hours. Stop wasting your hours. You win!

And this leads me to my next point. (I love when it works out this way!)

## Strip Away Complexity

I love simplicity. I love small words. I love tiny sentences. (Thank you, E. Annie Proulx.) The truth is that most of our lives are built around simplicity; we humans are the ones who try to make it more complex.

Sometimes, we do this out of fear. I've had businesspeople tell me about their business using a lot of words and citing a lot of processes. It's clear that they're afraid that I (or a prospective customer) am not going to think what they do is worth it, or important, or difficult. A lot of times, this weird defensiveness creeps into our lives when we worry that someone else will perceive our contributions as being too simple.

But how much of life and business is really that simple?

Look back a few pages (or rewind the audio) to the point where we discussed business models. Did you see how simply we talked about them? Actually, go ahead and reread *any* page in this book. Simple is one of the best and most powerful kinds of magic out there.

As Steve Jobs stated his goal: Put a thousand songs in your pocket.

So—how simply can *you* talk about your business? It's a strong challenge. When I launched *Owner*, I wanted to make it clear that we were a business magazine, but one that catered more to the how-to of the future of business than something that just covers the stories of the day. James Altucher summed it up when he said, "Oh, it's the business curriculum for the future." Pow. Just like that. Easy.

My challenge to you in *all* things is to make it simpler, even if it's just the background of your business. For instance, while Cirque du Soleil is anything *but* simple, it's really simple to describe: it's an upscale circus. All that complexity goes into its production, not into the business structure around it. Make sense?

From here, let's move into plotting out some kind of skeletal structure for how you build and operate your business. This is more of that "serving suggestion" information and "jumping off point" talk that I mentioned earlier in this chapter, but I'm hoping it's enough to give you a direction and some good ideas.

Let's frame up your days so you can think through how this will really work for you.

# 5 Fall in Love with Not Knowing

Here's a typical conversation with Rob Hatch, president of Owner Media Group:

Me: I think we should launch a magazine.
Rob: Do we know how to do that?
Me: It'll be digital. Kind of like a blog, but I dunno . . . more.
Rob: Well, let's do it!

This wasn't always the way. A few years ago, Rob would say things more like "Maybe we should think about this for a while." To which I'd reply, "I just bought the domain and ordered the software." Rob has eventually come to the realization that we're going to learn how to do whatever we're about to do midway through. And I've come to learn to actually wait until Rob says okay before I start something new (most times, anyway).

Not everyone feels that way. They want the details. They want to be well versed. They feel that they must have every angle covered before they plunge into the fray.

Further, a great many people are deathly afraid of being seen making mistakes or, worse, failing. The worst thing in the universe would be to not have the answer to a question a customer or client might ask. A lot of times, this comes from some great childhood experience, either at school or at home (or both), where someone made you feel horrendous for any one of the following reasons:

- Not knowing an answer.
- Trying something and not succeeding.
- Guessing incorrectly.
- Making a mistake.

Of course, if you're reading this book, whatever you did back then evidently didn't kill you. I'll go on record hoping that it didn't kill or permanently damage anyone else. Thus, you hereby have my 100 percent absolution for making mistakes and not knowing things. Yep. Free of charge. All for you. (I'm sorely tempted to put in a rip-out coupon for you to frame or keep in your purse or wallet.)

## Everything We Know How to Do Starts with *Not Knowing* How to Do It

We were not born walking. We were not born talking. Everything we do comes from *figuring it out*. It's strange that some of us become paralyzed with fear over not knowing what to do. *It's okay*. It's how everything works.

Through interviewing several interesting freaks and entrepreneurs for this book, I came repeatedly to the question of whether the person knew what they were doing before they started their project. The answers unanimously were, "Not really. I had a hunch or I had a related-but-not-the-same experience, but that's it."

The next section gives a good example.

### Roderick Russell: Sword Swallower

Roderick Russell knows *way* too much about coffee. I met up with him at the Speckled Ax in Portland, Maine; we were both speaking at the same conference the day before. He said to the barista behind the counter, "Tell me about your different origins." The fellow started to say something, but Roderick interrupted, "Wait, about the Sumatra. Are there any interesting characteristics or faults?"

How does he know all this? For one, he pays attention to the thoughts and opinions of the Specialty Coffee Association of America. He doesn't brew coffee. He doesn't grow it. He doesn't pour it at some restaurant. In the span of my asking about how he knew all that he did about coffee, this 30-something sword swallower, mind reader, stage hypnotist, and speaker told me about all the aspects that affect the flavor of coffee—altitude, weather, how the berries are washed and dried, and more. I reviewed my interview with him maybe 12 times and could have written a how-to guide for appreciating the taste of coffee instead of this book. His talk was *that* detailed.

And yet, when I asked him how one becomes a sword swallower, Roderick said that one learns to do this by *starting to do* it.

"Some people say they start by dangling cooked spaghetti down their throat to start numbing their gag reflexes. I believe that if you want to swallow swords, you practice by swallowing swords."

Clearly, one doesn't know how to do this until they learn. Roderick learned by practicing and trying, and gaining a quarter inch of depth at a time until he could get the sword all the way into his throat to the hilt of the blade. But it was always a quarter inch at a time.

Can you apply this to choices you intend to make about the work you intend to do? Of course!

## Try It

Depending on the idea or project or business plan, you can usually find a way to try a variation or version of the project before you commit yourself fully to the path of doing something more drastic. For instance, if your day job is at a real estate firm, but you've always wanted to launch your own gourmet cookie business, you can start practicing what it means to prepare a greater number of cookies than "a few dozen for the school bake sale." You can begin working out what that costs up front, and maybe rent space in a certified kitchen (these are popping up everywhere as a way for food people to "lab" their ideas).

Try some smaller version of the project. As Roderick Russell points out, though, do what you can to make the trial something that closely resembles the real effort you intend to perform. If you want to be a public speaker, starting by recording YouTube videos is great. However, you might also try to get yourself booked for some freebies at the local library or Rotary Club or something so that you can test out speaking in front of a live crowd.

## Want to Know Something? Ask Good Questions

Kate White is a multi-time *New York Times* best-selling author and speaker who also took over *Cosmopolitan* magazine (and related properties) back in 1998 and brought much success to the organization along the way. I had the opportunity to interview her as promotion for one of her books. Afterward, I took a chance and asked her a few questions relating to my magazine.

I've come to learn this: Really smart and important people will answer your questions, provided:

- Your question is succinct enough to answer without a lot of hard work.
- The person believes you're actually going to *do something* with the information they give you.

Kate White gave me very useful advice and confirmed a lot of my own thoughts on the matter. She provided me with wisdom that I didn't have to acquire myself because I was willing to trust the source, and because I knew enough to recognize an answer that was really useful.

The lesson is simple: learn how to *ask better questions*.

I receive hundreds of e-mails a day, some number of which come from smart people asking me for advice or to weigh in with my relevant experience. I also get questions like "How can I become famous?" Hmmm. Well . . . I can't help but answer that kind of question without a silly or sarcastic answer.

Here are some ways to formulate and ask better questions:

- **Ask questions that match the person's expertise.** I'm asked quite often about SEO. I don't know the first thing about it; and if people had done proper research on me, they'd know this.
- **Ask questions that the other person can answer briefly enough, but that will give *you* something to do later.** For instance, I asked Kate White how I could go about building greater distribution for *Owner* magazine. Her response was to book myself for many more interviews, work on "viral pieces," do more video, and more.

**Ask questions to more than one person with similar expertise, but never ask someone to validate or retort someone else's answer.** Everyone sees things differently. If I asked Felix Dennis from Dennis publications (they produce *Maxim*, among many other magazines) for his take on what I should do with *Owner*, his answers might agree with Kate's experiences, but that's not the value of asking either person for their thoughts. You be the arbiter and judge of which advice works best for you. And one caution:

- **Never, ever, *ever* ask someone questions if the answers can easily be found by using Google search and/or YouTube.** It's great to get a different perspective, but if you're asking rather simple, 101-type questions, you're likely to never get the chance to ask something ever again.

Another method I sometimes use, especially when asking people more general questions, is to ask a lot of people a *very similar question* so that I can get a lot of opinions then sort through the responses to find the similarities among the responses.

Sometimes, I don't even ask a question out loud, but I'll have a question in mind when I attend a conference and hear people's speeches. While listening to what the person is saying, I'll keep my thoughts in two places: both listening and thinking of the question I will ask. Sometimes, the person on stage answers my question without even knowing that I asked (kind of).

One final word of caution before we find another way to tackle not knowing: Sometimes, people use questions as a means of procrastination. Know whether that's your angle. If so, stop.

## One Good Way to Get Answers Is to Figure It Out

I had little publishing experience when I launched *Owner* magazine. I had never built a magazine before. I didn't have an editorial process in place to manage my authors. I had an idea how "real" magazines did "ads," but knew that's not what I wanted, so I started trying to figure out more creative ways to build partnerships with brands instead of just asking them to pay for banner and link space in my magazine.

If you want to know more than you did, just launch something and see what happens. Obviously, you might not be able to do this completely or all the time. If you want to try a 6,000-mile journey, you might have to figure out a smaller bite of your trial. But most times, you can do *something* that will get you started on the learning.

A while back, I taught some businesspeople how to blog. They worked for really big companies with well-known brands—so it was important that we practiced first before launching into a public blog. So I helped them by starting a blog about a topic that had nothing to do with their business (we chose poker), and then I showed them how to create accounts to write on the blog (we used fake names for the sake of the exercise). This allowed these people to try out blogging, see what happens when people comment, and learn how people respond and react to posts and information. They essentially tried everything they needed to learn by doing the actual act instead of listening to someone talk about it or just reading about it.

## Some Things Are Unknowable

"How will it turn out?" That's a reasonably unknowable detail, don't you agree? We can, however, understand and prepare for the challenges we'll face. Many people opt not to be freaks and instead do what needs doing when they reach a point where the outcome or answer is too nebulous.

At an event the other day, I asked a young lady how she went from being passionate about singing to a job in marketing. She said, "Well, you have to have a plan B, and I guess this just is what I'm doing right now." I asked her why she didn't pursue plan A. Her response: "Because how would I know if I succeeded?"

Hint: 100 percent of the attempts you choose *not* to make will net you 100 percent in the loss column.

The unknowable is an opportunity. It means that it's not a no. There's always a chance (speaking of that: http://hbway.com/chance).

## Be Willing to Be Dumb and Wrong

One of our biggest fears as businesspeople and professionals is being caught unaware. We hate seeming dumb, and we're not all that happy when we're wrong. Dumb is just another way of saying ignorant.

And ignorance is beautiful, because it means you don't know something. There's an implied "yet" to the concept of ignorance. The smartest people I know are ignorant. They shrug and smile and dig into what needs figuring out. They say "I have no idea" as fast as they can. And then they set out to learn. Being dumb just means you don't have the scoop, or have a little more work to do. Dumb, as it turns out, can be cured.

Stupid, however, is that problem where people have closed their mind off to any more learning. Stupid is what we are when we try to defend against others thinking we don't know something. You *can't* cure stupid.

A close cousin to being dumb is being wrong. If you're willing to be wrong, and willing to accept that you're wrong (and hopefully, no one gets hurt by your wrongness), you can cover a lot of ground that others will be avoiding.

## How to Be Wrong

There are probably some ways to be wrong that are better than others, and some steps that help you be wrong in a more constructive way. Being wrong is a great element of not knowing.

- If you're wrong and it hurts someone else, apologize. Of course, you should try never to hurt others, but when you do, be really clear with your apology. The best apologies have what we call the "Three A's."
  - **Acknowledge.** Acknowledge that you made a mistake.
  - **Apologize.** Apologize clearly and simply: "I'm sorry."
  - **Act.** Do something that will help eradicate the chances of being wrong and hurting someone in the same way again.
- If you are wrong and it hurts you and/or your business, do an "after-action report." Write out what happened, how it happened, and what you might do to ensure it *doesn't* happen again.
- If you are wrong but you learn a lot from it, smile. This is a big deal. I've invested a lot in my mistakes. When I learn from what has gone wrong, I know I've gotten an education.
- If you are wrong but you figure out how to save other people some time, you've just picked up another magical superpower for your freaky entrepreneurial power collection. Because helping others not repeat something you did wrong is valuable. It increases your worth.

Wrong is such an awesome opportunity, provided no one is hurt. It's one of the best schools I've ever attended. Throw a lot of dumb into the mix, and you are cooking with gas. But if all you ever do is correct your mistakes and sit around being dumb, you're not pushing hard enough.

## Curiosity Gets Such a Bad Rap (R.I.P., Cat)

One way to really amp up your smarts and really deliver great value to yourself is to be curious and to seek out knowledge wherever you can find it.

Curiosity fuels passion like you wouldn't believe. It allows your mind to see things from different angles. And the very best news is this: your brain gets a workout whether or not you are learning about something that relates to your business.

But only if you do something to keep strengthening those particular mental muscles—and *only* if you do so actively.

## Explore So Much That You Make Dora Look Like a Homebody

When it comes to not knowing, you can have a field day by looking into all kinds of new and interesting areas. By learning new things, your brain opens up new pathways. I'll give you a reasonably random example.

A year or so ago, I watched a documentary film called *Happy* (http://thehappymovie.com). I learned that there are more 100-year-olds per capita in Okinawa, an island in Japan, than anywhere else in the world. The people who live there embrace a concept where Okinawans care for each other as if they are all *one family*. Beyond flesh and blood, there are several rituals that reinforce this idea of helping to build connections and value the connectedness of people.

I learned the word *monchu*, which means, "one family." It turns out that this word isn't part of the Japanese language; it is unique to Okinawa. And it took me watching a documentary about happiness, and seeing a bunch of over-100-year-old ladies bonding with each other and kids and praising the value of having lots of friends that I learned how very important a *monchu* can be.

The term *monchu* is something I'm now teaching everyone who reads *Owner* magazine. I took something that I learned just by watching a film out of curiosity and made it central to my business plans. If you ask anyone in business—heck, just let me ask *you!*— "Does networking work?" What do you get for an answer? If you hear "yes," run away from the person who tells you that. If *you* said yes, you'll have to tell me how it has worked for you.

*Monchu* means "one family" and embodies the concept that you could help to build value for everyone around you. *Networking* means, What can you do for me today?

Which do you want to promote? Which will deliver value for you over time? Which will give you some superpowers?

Curiosity. Superpower. Magic. Try new things. Learn new things. Learn what else you don't know. Learn tons more than the other person about whatever makes your senses tingle.

## The Secret Prison of Not Knowing "Regular" Stuff

There's a weird experience that happens to me often. It goes something like this: I'll get an e-mail from a follower that states "Chris, I've decided I want to build a business on the Internet, so I'm taking a course about HTML and a course about web design, and I'm learning Photoshop, and I'm going to build my own website."

At that moment, I reply, "Why not just build the site using WordPress, pay a designer to make it pretty—and then just do the business work?"

The answer back is often something about "figuring I should know." But that's a bit like saying you're interested in baking muffins and learning metallurgy to create the muffin tins.

This chapter instructs you to fall in love with *not knowing*. There's a safety measure to this, as well. Oftentimes, we get too deep into the thinking and planning and learning and researching and *we don't execute*. Back when I was trying to write fiction books, I would fill notepads with "backstory" and "character development," but I wouldn't actually write the stories. If you're not doing the work, you're not doing the work.

If everyone around you is learning to master the accounting code, there are two possibilities: (1) You all need to know it, so mastery is table stakes, and therefore it doesn't count, so just learn it; or (2) you don't need to know it at all, but because others are studying it, you think you should, too.

When social media first came out, people seemed to feel you had to be on every social network, whether or not you liked it—and whether or not you could keep up with posting everywhere. Hundreds and hundreds of social networks sprung up, thus crushing everyone's ability to do that. Meanwhile, folks who stuck to one or two or three networks managed to build communities they could sustain, and derived some level of value from their efforts.

Advice:

- Study something far afield of what everyone else in your business finds interesting.
- Avoid doing what the guy beside you is doing. As a freak, this shouldn't be too difficult for you. But don't ever think you have to do something just because someone else is doing it—or because everyone else is doing it.
- Determine what "just enough" knowledge looks like, and save your studying for the weird and curious and passionate opportunities you can pursue.

## Testing and Stats and Analytics: My Story of Not Knowing

*He gets on base a lot. Do I care if it's a walk or a hit?*
—Brad Pitt as Billy Beane in *Moneyball*

I really loved the movie *Moneyball*. It tells the story of how manager Billy Beane took the Oakland Athletics to an incredible 20 consecutive wins by following the advice of a whiz kid statistics expert. They did this by finding *one* very specific stat that ends up doing the best job of predicting success: on-base average. The message: When you can really focus on a particular element, you can make great strides.

Since that movie, I've really pushed hard to keep only one or two metrics in mind for all aspects of my business. When I was planning *Owner*'s growth, I wanted the number of subscribers and the dollars in revenue to be those stats. If I get more subscribers, it means that I'm doing well at promoting the magazine and that people are sticking around. If I'm getting more money from my business partners and sponsors, it's because I'm delivering a value they appreciate.

That's it. Those are my stats: subscribers and revenue. I can measure just those two things and have a really good sense of what's going on.

But when I dive a little deeper, I learn a lot more. When I assess an element like bounce rate—that is, how long someone stays on a site before leaving again—I discover that people stick around only for two minutes or so and then leave. When I look at *that* even more deeply, it takes most people two minutes or less to read a 500-word post, and that's the chosen length of most of our posts on *Owner*.

Then I have to ask myself, "What do I really want that stat to mean to me?" In my specific case, I don't care. So I throw that stat away. Instead, I look for something more relevant. For instance, if I can see where they click after they read my article, that'll tell me whether or not my calls to action are worth it. That kind of ability, knowing which stats to keep and which to ignore, becomes important. It'll be different in your business, naturally, but I think there's value in thinking through every number you're inclined to keep and why.

See how complex you can make things if you try? People looking at how they'd like to do business have an interesting challenge of figuring out which stats to measure and how to make them matter or not. For instance, artists tend not to value their time when they price their pieces.

Maybe it takes you two hours to make an amazing duct-tape wallet that you sell for $10. That means that you have paid yourself less than $5 an hour, after you account for the cost of materials. If you measure only sales revenue, maybe you'll be happy when you sell $100 worth of product. Meanwhile, it took you 20 hours to produce those wallets. Twenty hours, or half of a work week, to make $100? Ouch.

## Not Knowing versus Not Thinking Something Through

We've just uncovered a different kind of not knowing: not *thinking*. A lot of the time, this falls into the being ignorant/dumb camp; and that's okay. It doesn't take long to account for this.

In her book *I Shouldn't Be Telling You This*, Kate White calls this "draining the swamp instead of just killing the alligators." Translation: Don't just take care of the little chores that seem to keep piling up. Dig deeper to see whether perhaps some process or system or other circumstance isn't causing these to grow.

Build a process for looking over how you're doing what you're doing. We'll cover this deeper in Chapter 8, "Create Systems That Work for You." But don't wait for that. Take a note. Write down "swamp/alligators" and make sure that we fall in love with not knowing, but that we don't accidentally dumb ourselves into a corner by not looking things over from time to time.

## A Fun Project

People have a weird habit of writing "Someday, I'm going to learn more about this or that" kinds of lists. These lists look great, don't they? But no one ever crosses off the items on their "someday" list. You could stun me and be the first, but let's not be crazy. Instead, how about this: Write out five things you've always been a bit curious about. Right now. I'll wait.

Okay, are you back?

Now, Google them. (Hey, you have to start somewhere.) Is there anyone you know who is involved in what you are interested about, or has something to do with it? Follow them on Twitter or find them on LinkedIn. Look around for a meetup. Watch a show about the subject. Whatever. But do *something* that you've never done and don't know anything about. Learn something new. And try *not* to make it something that really relates to your business plans, okay?

This chapter was about how what you don't know is awesome. The next chapter? It's the most beautiful line ever drawn in the sand: the difference between a freak who knows what she wants and will make it happen, and a wonderful person who will surrender to the whims of the world. It's about doing the work and loving it.

Smell that? It's your victory. And it comes from learning to accept and enjoy obstacles and challenges.

# 6 Structure a Framework for Your Days

**W**hat did you do when you woke up this morning? If you're like most people, you reached for your phone and checked your e-mail (and tweets and other messages). First thing. Even before you went pee. Lots of people sleep with their phone only a few inches from their head, as if they were a brain surgeon or a superhero awaiting that *very important* call. (Some people have that kind of mission-critical life. I don't envy them.) But why do they do that first?

Answer: They do it out of habit.

No matter what justification you're going to give me (I have to see if something is blowing up), it's a habit. It's a learned behavior.

What did you do after looking in your inbox or at your texts? I'm betting you reacted to something there and took an action based on what you found there. You followed a response pattern.

Sadly, you and I and lots of people serve these two bosses more than any other: *habits and reactions.*

Just let that one sink in for a second. Do you agree? Okay, but now let's turn this on its end.

If you picked better habits, and chose reactions that served you, wouldn't that be a *good* thing? I sure think so. *Structure* is based on your ability to create and follow patterns—which then become habits—and to respond to your environment after bouncing that response against your plans. Make sense?

## Structure Gets a Bad Rap

When we think about trying to put a little more structure into our days, the freak in us likes to rebel. "But wait! I'm not a robot. I'm not built to just execute programs like that." And yet, a lot of what we do during most days is built on habits and reactions, which are basically scripts that we operate without a whole lot of conscious thought. Programs.

But structure is just a way to establish a framework that allows you to build what you want to build. A haiku is a structure, but the payload of the effort is unique. A TV show is built differently from a movie: If you tried to use a movie's framework for a TV show, it wouldn't work.

When I write a book, I use a structure. If I didn't, it would just amble all over the place with no intent or purpose (hush, critics!). When I give a speech, even if there are no slides, I follow a structure and a path. Sometimes, that's just a three-by-five card with a bulleted list that tells the story I need to tell. But without it, I'm prone to go off course and off topic.

## Cure Your Procrastination

One reason we delay actions is that we don't really know what we should be doing, or what comes next.

What if you had a framework for every task that you needed to accomplish, and a few items to do under each of those tasks? For instance, let's say I've got some sales calls to make. I'm nervous about sales; I dislike rejection as much as the next freak. So I have a list of five steps. It looks like this:

1. Send the next e-mail.
2. Agree upon goals.
3. Set the date.

4. Invoice.
5. Do the actual work.

It's so simple. It's that which needs to be done. As I'm typing this, I have to accomplish these five items for a specific project I'm working on. Let's call this the simplest and most basic framework: *the list*.

## Fear and Procrastination

On the day I wrote this part, I received some really icky business-related news. I ended up opening all the letters, reading all the assertions, and then understanding the next steps I had to pursue to solve the issue in the coming days.

Had this all happened a few years ago, I would have put off even opening the mail for a few weeks—maybe a few months. I would have avoided it. Back then, I was choosing fear over taking action—and that fear simply bred more procrastination. That's a lot of what our fears do: keep us from taking an action, even if the action is as seemingly simple as gathering more information.

So here's the challenge for *you*: From now on, when fear sets you on the path of procrastination, choose instead to take the next step of gathering some information. You don't even have to take an *action* yet. Just gather a few more facts and ask a few more questions: "What might happen next? What are the options?"

But that's just some path-clearing to think about. First, we have to talk about making sure that what we do will push us in the direction of our larger goals. Then, we'll work through a structure for your typical days, plus a few other types of days.

## Develop a Long View: Our Days Must Serve Our Weeks and Our Weeks Must Serve Our Larger Goals

The easiest way to fail is to think in terms of the "day" as the standard unit of measurement. If you *plan* day to day, you'll never do anything particularly big—because the "big" work of your plans usually requires a bit more work than can normally fit into 24 hours. You have to develop a longer view.

Let's use goals as a unit of measurement. To build a long view, you need goal markers set up at these distances:

- Five years
- Three years
- One year
- Six months
- Three months
- One month
- One week

It would be overly simple to believe you can start at the top of this set of markers and then just fill it in downward. For instance, if your five-year goal is to have your incredible organic candy bar company set up with a nationwide (soon to be international) presence, but your goal for one month is to be able to pay the rent and bills without dipping into your credit card, it's going to take a little bit of tweaking to make those pieces connect and make sense.

The truth is that your bottom three (or four) goal markers will always shift a bit. And sometimes, everything will go out the window entirely. But having these in place will help you a lot more than *not* having them.

Let me fill these in with an older version of my goals (not what I'm currently doing) as an example:

- Five years: Acquired at a $10 million payout.
- Three years: Steady $5 million in revenue.
- One year: 100,000 subscribers to my newsletter.
- Six months: 50,000 subscribers to my newsletter.
- Three months: Courses in place.
- One month: Courses shaped up.
- One week: Work on courses and subscribers.

This example explains my previous business model: primarily selling courses. I had goals for subscribers and related revenue goals, and a future goal of being acquired by someone who would want the assets I'd created. A few other goals snuck into all these areas; this is just one version.

But the real trick is for *you* to identify milestones you want to hit and fill out the goals on this time line for yourself—and use it in any way you want. Here's how it would look if you focused on goals for your health.

- Five years: Steady state management of health and fitness.
- Three years: Optimal weight for two years.
- One year: Complete a marathon.
- Six months: Six pants sizes down.
- Three months: Three pants sizes down.
- One month: Gym three times a week.
- One week: Drink my body weight in ounces of water daily; walk briskly daily.

Once you have a rough idea of your goal, the milestones are easy to identify. The mind-set I'm working on imparting is the notion that you can't work on the day to day until you've got something a little more solidly in play for your future goals and vision. Make sense? Now fill this in for yourself:

- Five years:
- Three years:
- One year:
- Six months:
- Three months:
- One month:
- One week:

And with this in mind, let's go through some of what you need to succeed day to day. You might have to make some changes, but let's start here.

## A Daily Framework

Here's a sample of what you could create for yourself to help tackle the challenges you'll face, whether you're the employeepreneur still working for a boss, a solo owner, or the leader of a team or company. In any scenario, this will provide a way to keep yourself focused and pointed in the right direction.

| Three-Month Goal | | Contacts Today | |
|---|---|---|---|
| Week's Big Goal | | | |
| Must Do Today | | | |
| Must Do Today | | | |
| Must Do Today | | Reach Out List | |
| Mantra Today | | | |
| Watch Out for | | | |
| The Prize Is | | | |

You can make this list look a lot cooler. You could jot this into your paper notebook, or put something like this in your Evernote, or whatever method you like best.

Start by jotting down your three-month goal at the top of your daily list. It will help you remember the larger story and where you're headed. If that's still too soon, use your one-year goal. If you ever worry about straying from the path, that little reminder will keep you working on what's important.

The week's big goal is also self-explanatory, but it's a way to keep your mind really pointed in the right direction. Skip writing this down daily and you'll think that the week is something you can waste, or that you can make it up later. But the fact is that you rarely get the opportunity to make up for wasted time.

Then determine the three items—maybe even six, if you're feeling ambitious—that you must do today. Lists fail us when we overload them and then get excited that we get some of the items on the list done, but miss the rest. Do you think that feeling that it's okay to *not* finish your list is a good idea?

The concept of "mantra today" is based on a lot of practice, the help of my girlfriend, Jacqueline Carly, cofounder and editor-in-chief of *BossFit* magazine, and the countless interviews I've read from successful people who say that they work with a mantra of some kind to fuel their success. Without diverting your attention from the rest of the list, let's use the term *mantra* in this case to refer to "instructions you give yourself repeatedly to reset your thoughts and clear your frustrations." A mantra isn't the same as an affirmation, which is basically a positive statement that you use to encourage yourself. Instead, it's something we say to help us stop thinking about unnecessary stuff and reset our attention onto our goals.

So answer this question: What would get you to shake yourself out of a rut or a bad mood or a wrong spot, and put you back on a path of productive work? It doesn't have to be fancy. It can be a prayer. It can be whatever. Just don't invest in the very words of the mantra. Invest in the practice of learning to "stop, reset." That's the trick.

## What Not to Do

We have used to-do lists on and off all our lives. But have you ever used a "*not* to-do" list? I refer to this as a "watch out for" list. Example: When I'm frustrated, I like to eat something bad for me. That messes with my health goals, though it helps my stress goals. I might say "Watch out for: stress eating" as a way to remind myself to have a big glass of water, do a quick burst of jumping jacks or take a quick brisk walk, and try to fix two issues at once.

For your "prize" you can use this in a couple of different ways: one, reward yourself in some way every single day. Two, remind yourself about what you're really working toward and how the work you're doing will serve that. For instance, if you're looking to go from being deeply in debt to living debt-free, maybe the prize is "working 20 days a month max." It's up to you. Heck, maybe you want to glue a picture in that spot.

Now, the right column is split in two: Who do you have to contact today to advance your business? That's the easy one. The second list—the "reach out list"—are people to contact whom you can help, who can mentor you, whom you value, and so forth, but who aren't directly involved with your business needs. Does the difference make sense? You've got to contact certain people to do your business; the second column involves the individuals who matter to you *beyond* the business in some way. That's the list for a typical day. You might add or subtract an item or two—but it's a starting point to jump-start your thinking. Have you ever worked with a list anything like this? Have you done so daily?

# Commit to Working for Two Months with a List

It doesn't have to be the exact list that I offer in this chapter, but I want you to commit right now to spending two months to daily use of a checklist. The list should advance your goals as an owner, and help you to get from where you are to where you intend to go next. Can you make that commitment?

Okay, presuming you just said yes (because I'll hunt you down and challenge you more if you don't), let's look at a few other ways to create some lists and some variations, and what they might offer for your business.

## A List of Lists of Awesomeness (or Helpfulness)

**Decision list:** This list is so simple, yet, sometimes, it can be very powerful.

| Reasons Why | Reasons Why Not |
| --- | --- |
| | |

This table could also be titled "Good/Bad" or "Stay/Go" or whatever you choose. Sometimes called the "T-bar list," this is the very classic pros and cons kind of list. You essentially count up how many ideas fit in the left column versus the right column to help you make decisions.

**Someday/maybe list:** This list is right out of David Allen's *Getting Things Done*, and it's a list where you put ideas you might want to pursue in the future, or tasks that won't be good for you to pursue right now. I have one variant for using this list, however. Once you fill it out, throw it in the trash or burn it in the fire. You don't have time to wait to do this someday. Work on it now.

**Value/worth list:** This is one of the tools to use if you're the type of person who likes to spend money. I use something like this quite often to determine whether I'm being financially careless, and to remind myself of better goals. The following table gives some examples.

| One | Costs | Per Month | Per Year | Versus |
|-----|-------|-----------|----------|--------|
| Latte | $ 4 | 80 (20 days) | $ 960 | Trip to CA |
| Dinner out | $50 (solo) | 200 (4x/month) | $2,400 | Trip to EUR |
| Spotify | $10 | 10 | $ 120 | MP3s |

In the first two examples I could buy an airplane ticket to California (from Boston) instead of having a latte every day, and a ticket to Europe and back instead of eating out once a week. Obviously, the "versus" category can be other items or experiences you're hoping to acquire. In my last example, I justify Spotify because it'd cost a heck of a lot less than buying individual albums via MP3 (musicians, yes, I do know that Spotify pays you pocket lint).

This list is *really* helpful in thinking through all kinds of solutions. Should you rent office space instead of getting your kids to give you some free space in the basement? At $300/month (being conservative), that's $3,600 a year. That same money could buy you a . . . what? In the reverse, maybe you're thinking about heading down to that cool tech conference and you've figured out that it costs about $3,600 all-in. Is that event more important than an office away from the house? (See how this works?)

*Monchu* list: Remember, *monchu* means "one family"; I use it to refer to "people who are important to you, but aren't necessarily part of your bloodline." Similar to your Reach-Out List in the daily framework, this is a concept for a list of 20 people (maybe a few less) that you contact often. Maybe not daily, but often enough to keep the relationship warm. Not clients, but people you can help, who might be able to help you—the individuals who make your world better. This one is probably the hardest to accomplish, and yet it's very useful.

**Master "not-to-do" list:** There are many tasks and chores and habits and repeat experiences you tend to find yourself doing. I know because I do it too. For instance, if I get really exasperated, I'll try to create a new method of organizing, even though organization is never really part of the problem. I also check Twitter incessantly when I'm procrastinating on doing something very important (like making a sales call). So I have a few not-to-do lists—one of which I keep close to my field of vision by my computer.

**People-to-meet list:** This seems silly, and yet, it's not. Having a list of the people you hope you meet means you can work on ways to make it real. I have this list. On it are Sir Richard Branson, author William Gibson (author), and Scarlett Johansson (hey, why not?). Who would be on yours?

**Big-dream list:** On this might go "Play the Royal Albert Hall" or "Be a *New York Times* best-selling author" (hey, I did that!), or "Buy an ocean-front house in the Caribbean." This list can be an amazing opportunity, especially if you become daring and try to find ways to make this list tie in with your goal-marker list and, thus, your daily list. It's up to you, though. Feeling a bit crazy? Write out this list.

# But Frameworks Aren't All Lists: Habits and More

We all have habits, as I said at the top of the chapter. We need more habits than follow a framework. So let's go through some of those here.

**Think in terms of "Mortgage Math."** I have a lot of little calculations I do when it comes to money. For instance, when I launched the opportunity for people to advertise in my newsletter, I decided there would be three slots for $500 each at launch—$1,500 per issue times four issues a month equals $6,000. If I sell all the spots, I can pay four times my mortgage every month (around $1,400). Similarly, if I'm pursuing something that becomes a hassle, I ask whether it's worth the money—and I use my mortgage math to think about it. This can help you plot some of the rabbit holes you choose to visit in a given day.

**Make meetings micro.** If you want more time, accept only brief meetings. You might assume that you can't make this happen if you're the employee—but you can. I once had a boss who taught me how to hold 20-minute meetings—fast, powerful, can't-miss events for those involved in the project. Word got around that we were getting a lot done in these 20-minute meetings. You can bet the culture changed a bit after that.

**Value your synchronous time.** There should be a sliding scale on the value you place on meetings and time. For instance, someone asks me for an interview, I ask them to send the questions via e-mail. There's no value to me in talking to someone over the phone and waiting for them to write down my answers (which also runs the risk of them misquoting me). Real time is expensive and should be your least-used method of taking care of business that doesn't require it.

**Say no. A lot.** I know I've mentioned this already, but it's so crucial that I'm saying it again. Early on in my business, I often said "Yes, because what if . . ." to requests I knew were silly. I also said yes a lot because I didn't want to seem like a jerk by having to decline something. But you *never get time back*—and other people aren't going to volunteer to do your work for you. If you say yes to something just to be nice, you miss being able to say yes to what's important to you.

**Plan your schedule at 40 percent.** This is a new concept for me. When you plan your schedule full to the top, something inevitably goes wrong. That's when you need more time to fix a problem. If you plans your life so that only about 40 percent of your hours were scheduled, you'll have some extra time and energy to put toward the problems that pop up. If nothing's going wrong, you can always do something unscheduled during that time. But if you take on more and more scheduled work, you'll eventually drown in it.

## What Comes Next?

The following chapters are patterned like "Choose Your Own Adventure" stories. These allow me to specifically address the kind of owner you might be. If you're an employeepreneur, I give you some ideas that speak to that. A solo owner or a very small business? I have something for you. Are you an owner who's been at it a while and yet are still a freak inside? I've got a chapter for you.

# 7 Are You an Employeepreneur?

This question is meant to determine if this chapter is for you. If it's not, go ahead to the next chapter.

An *employeepreneur* is someone who has a job in a company, but is executing it like an owner. They have a stronger interest in the business's outcomes than your average employee, and operates with the sense that they own and marshal the resources around them. This means you get a paycheck from someone. You're an employee. And yet, you think of yourself as a boss (not in that cool "like a boss!" way—http://hbway.com/likeaboss).

Don't confuse this with the sometimes-labeled "wantrepreneur"—someone with a day job seeking to exit their company to run their own business at some point. Whether or not that's true of you, I'm speaking to you in this chapter as if you're *happy* with the day job; you simply seek to build a better interface between your different mind-sets and the way business might be done in your organization.

## What a Boss Wants

Employeepreneurs usually find themselves working through their own ambitions and goals, which is great and expected. However, because you're under someone else's employ, it's your responsibility to serve that person to the best of your abilities. It's never ever useful to be at odds with your leadership's larger goals, even if you're forever striving to change how they get there. Said another way, the only path for an employeepreneur is to serve your leadership through your actions.

Bosses want results without a lot of friction. They want action without a lot of interaction. They want to be informed, and never caught off guard. They want your actions to make them shine without upstaging them. Oftentimes, they want to get home and leave the office/workplace behind.

Did that last one surprise you? Once, a long while back, I came into my boss's office with great ambition. I'd had a breakthrough idea, I felt, and I knew that it would be something really exciting for our company to pursue. I decided to pitch it to the man who could make it happen.

The boss, never one to make a lot of eye contact, stared at his screen while I presented my idea. He seemed to listen, to appreciate my thoughts. He said something noncommittal (which wasn't out of the norm), and as I headed out of the office, I noticed that what was on his screen was a picture of a BMW and a picture of a Mercedes. He was doing some kind of purchasing comparison.

Now, the interesting part of the story is that he ended up taking my recommendations. He backed the project, and my idea turned out to be really helpful in a small way. But I never once forgot my realization that he wasn't focused on innovation and the future of the company every waking minute, the way I was. And that wasn't bad or wrong; he just had different priorities and was at a different point in his career.

**The huge takeaway:** It doesn't matter. If you're passionate and ambitious and the boss isn't, provided you can do the bulk of the work and get the support you need, who cares? The magic still happens. But remember: not everyone shares your nutty ambitions.

## *The Matrix* (the Movie, That Is) and You

If I had my corporate life to do over again, I would redo so much. I used to get mired in every possible distraction. I was far too social with my coworkers, was way too deeply involved in office politics, and spent much too much time worrying over really stupid and petty issues. As a result, I burned a bunch of years failing to advance and acquire the power to make my time in corporate life as valuable as it could have been. In short, I fell into the Matrix.

To explain the analogy: The movie *The Matrix* sets up a world in which all reality as we know it is just a massive virtual-reality program, and we humans are all dormant and plugged into giant robotic farms that suck the life out of us as if we were batteries. The takeaway is that there's a fake world that we have all bought into. Certain people "wake up" and get unplugged from the Matrix, but then use other methods to plug back in and challenge the keepers of this oppressive system.

Stated much more succinctly, there's a lame reality that makes you docile and complacent; and then there's a way to wake up and do something really important and more "real."

We'll use the term *Matrix* to indicate all those not-really-important issues that get in our way in our working world—the things that keep us from working on the much more important issues. For instance, "Anja's chair is better than mine" is a Matrix issue. "Avinash is advancing much faster than me, and I suspect that it's because he's playing golf with the boss" is a Matrix issue.

We can get stuck in other people's lives. I realize now in hindsight that if I had spent a lot more time *working on my work*—and less time worrying about other people's dramas—things would have gone so much better for me in my old roles.

So instead of worrying about which offices your colleagues are assigned, focus on what you *can make happen*. Figure out how you can make progress that benefits your company, your boss, and you (though maybe the order should be your boss, your company, and you).

## Communication and Word Choice

If you want to become more influential as an employeepreneur almost immediately, one skill worth honing is your ability to *communicate better*. In this case, "better" simply means "succinctly, with positive word choices, and with more actionable results in mind." Let's break that down.

## Brevity Is the Gold Standard in Business

We tend to overwrite and overspeak everything in business—usually out of fear. We use way too many words in order to justify some choice or thought. People in business overcommunicate more often than not. This abundance of words usually leads to *under*communicating goals and intentions.

How do you put this goal into action? Let me give you four starting points just for today:

1. Make your subject line almost *more important* than the e-mail. (This is true in speaking with someone, too, only you say the subject line aloud as the first sentence.) So, for instance, send "Can we shorten standard meeting times?" instead of "Quick question" as your subject line. It immediately tells the person what you want to address.
2. Write your e-mails so they contain *no more than 350 words*. People don't have time. If you have to write something that is difficult to explain, consider writing a 350-word e-mail, and then writing the balance of the information below your signature.
3. If you have questions, consider only two formats: *one question per e-mail, or, a list of numbered questions*. The first is really effective in getting a clear and easy-to-understand response. The second is a way to get a bunch of information out of your recipient in a rapid-fire manner.
4. Consider phrasing your questions in a way that makes it easy for people to answer them definitively. "Where do you want to go to lunch?" is an invitation for 20 e-mails. "Are you up for lunch at that new Thai place?" will get you a yes or a no.

## Word Choice Is Mighty Important

One way you'll become an owner at work, even as an employeepreneur, is through your choice of words. If you just scoffed or felt this was cruddy advice, then skip this section. But if you're up for learning something, I'll give you three ideas that might really help.

1. **Always use the *most responsible words possible*.** That is, use the words that make it clear you own your spot at the time. Here's an example:
   - **Not claiming responsibility**: They wouldn't respond to my e-mail.
   - **Responsible**: I'm still nailing down their response.
   - **Not claiming responsibility**: My boss has me working on this project to rebuild our tagging.
   - **Responsible:** I'm leading a project to improve our tagging. Ownership starts with the words you use.
2. **No whining. Ever.** "I'm so busy." "My workload is crazy." Don't say it—people don't want to hear it.
3. **Use more positive words than negative words.** "I can't get the hang of this" becomes "I'm working on mastering this."

Does this connect with you? Do you understand it? I can tell you with certainty that people who choose their words better get further in their pursuits. Yes, it's what you're talking about that matters most, but it's also very much *how* you say it that will impact people's reactions to you.

This might have sounded a bit soft or inconsequential to you, but I promise it's not. It's not always *obvious* what makes one person earn advancements and grow through the ranks in an organization. However, I've observed a huge difference in how people perceive you and thus how they interact with you (and judge you) based on these kinds of details. Communication skills aren't an afterthought; they come right after your strategy and execution skills. If your work falls in the woods and no one's there, it won't make a sound.

## See Your Work Life as a Series of Projects

Lots of people have jobs that, if left as they were first conceived by the bosses, are kind of "steady-state" experiences: There is a desk and a list of tasks, and the boss just wants you to do that until you're dead (or find a new job). No matter how they framed it when you were hired—and no matter how others see it—it's ideal if you can consider your work experience as a series of projects.

This lets you segment and look for improvements, and decide how to use your time better. Even if you're a call-center rep with aspirations to fix the business (I was there!), the project mind-set will get you a lot further along. My call work was one project (the one I hoped to evade eventually). I took on a newsletter project. I did a Lotus 1-2-3 project to improve some processes. People saw me differently from the other call-center reps, which led to a promotion to management.

## Get the Exciting Projects

I used to wonder how certain people in my company would get all the plum job assignments. I thought they were maybe lucky, or maybe they were doing something shady—or bribing someone. It took me a while to learn that you get these projects by *earning your way there*.

There's a simple progression to how this happens, and it's outlined in these four steps.

1. **Accept and conquer small projects.** Your boss and colleagues will test you. Why would they give you something big if you can't even handle the little stuff? Take on and deliver small projects flawlessly and on time. Do extra work to make the projects even better somehow.
2. **Create your own projects.** People really dig it if you take the initiative and create a project that improves an aspect of the company in some way. I once revived a newsletter that had long been dormant at my company. The exposure earned me lots of other opportunities, while the project gave the management a way to communicate their messages, wrapped around the fun ways I built out the rest of the information. This led to more projects. Here's the trick: It must be a project that *improves the business*—even if just in a tiny way.

3. **Ask for crappy projects.** No one wants to do them for a reason: *because* they're crappy. But if you tackle them and win, you'll have helped the boss or your colleagues, and taken something off the collective plate. I used this approach repeatedly when I started as a project manager; it led other people to see me as someone who got things done. Then, instead of crappy projects, I took on the "in jeopardy" projects, and found I was able to deal with "burning train about to hit the brick wall" kinds of projects, and so I got lots of those. It was a great way to do the work I found the most exciting.

4. **Take on the bigger projects.** This is the reward for all your hard work. See what you can do when you finally get a big project. Hint: if you choke, that's probably not going to bode well for you. But if you work and earn the victory, you'll kick butt and be known as the kind of person who can execute huge projects and important work. How do you learn how to do this? Well, if my example's replicable, you just say yes to something, and then seek a little advice from peers and people who aren't your boss. Then use trial-and-error to make your way toward success.

## Do the Job That's in Front of You

Former U.S. Secretary of State and Chairman of the Joint Chiefs of Staff Colin Powell told a story in his first book, *My American Journey*, about mopping floors in the Coca-Cola bottling plant. The big boss—that is, the boss's boss's boss—came by and saw Powell mopping the floor with a great deal of attention to the quality of his work. When asked why he was tackling such a menial job with such intent, Powell replied that it was the job that was in front of him.

A lot of times, we have our eyes on some future role that currently isn't in our reach. It might *never* be something we can do at the company we're at; but that doesn't mean we should make a half-baked effort. One reason people find themselves without enough power to be an employeepreneur is because they scoff at the baseline work that comes with the role they occupy. Why would anyone give you a shot at something big if you're not giving attention to the primary role for which you were hired?

## Reject the "Not My Job" Mentality

The funniest misconception people have of what I do as an entrepreneur is that they believe there are "people" who do all kinds of work on my behalf. They believe someone else answers my e-mails (no, I do it). They think I have someone help me write my posts and books like this one (no, that's my job). If you're an entrepreneur, or an employeepreneur, you've got to embrace the realization that lots of work that maybe *shouldn't* be your job will still be part of the game.

The people who succeed are the ones who do the work that stands between them and their goal, no matter who owns it. That's actually what's at the heart of the entrepreneurial mind-set when one is an employee. Your goals are often beyond the scope of your work; you don't care what's technically your job and what isn't. (Note: If you ever do this in workplaces that have labor unions in place, you can run the risk of upsetting some people. Be careful about this.)

## Find Your Way to Your Goal

The "win" in being an employeepreneur is seeking out a goal and finding a way to accomplish it. More than one goal, most times. For instance, let's say you work in HR. You manage health benefits. Maybe you decide that you're going to implement a wellness project at work. The leadership decides they're into it, but don't want to fund it. The obstacle between you and your success is finding money for the project. How will you approach this? Where will you get the money? Poof. Welcome to the whole point of being an employeepreneur.

Stopping or seeing obstacles as the reason to quit are pretty much the opposite of the idea. Sure, you'll occasionally find that there isn't a viable solution. But that isn't a conclusion you should reach easily. There are always methods and ways that people overlook. What did you miss? Who else can help? Which resources haven't you thought to tap? Welcome to the fun of being a freak and an owner.

The next two chapters are for other types of owners. If you're an employeepreneur, you're not likely *also* someone running her own business; but maybe you are. You're probably not someone who's been an owner for quite a long while. If these roles don't apply to you, skip over them and tackle the following chapter. (But if you want to peek, who am I to stop you?)

# Create Systems That Work for You

logger, entrepreneur, and friend John Saddington recently made a public announcement to his community that he is dealing with autism, specifically Asperger's syndrome. Before I go much further, I should remind readers of the saying: If you've met one person with autism, you've met one person with autism. That is, everyone's different—and John's difference requires an interesting system.

John can remember things much better visually. Visual presentations stay with him much more clearly than audible ones; if John takes a picture, it will stick with him. For example, John would likely forget a grocery list's details, but if he photographs the list, he can navigate the store without a problem. He can remember people, but if he sees their photo, it's like opening up a mental database of what he knows about the person—even if they're just on the phone with him.

Because this is just how John is wired, he's developed a system to handle it best. And as a software entrepreneur, he's also created software to support that system. Pressgram (http://pressgr.am) is a photo-sharing software that lets you take photos on your smartphone and post them to WordPress. (If you're thinking "Like a private Instagram?" the answer is yes, but slightly different.) Pressgram makes a great alternative application where you control a lot more of the details—it allows you to do some very nuanced work.

So before we go on to talk about systems, think about how this story relates to the freaks concept. John's a freak just like you or me. His challenge is his autism, and building a business that he wants to build while living the life he wants to live. I can tell you that John's business is paying him well enough and he's living on his own terms, which sounds like success to me. The choices he's made have allowed him to inherit the earth he wants—specifically, his choice to *build systems* that work for him.

Why is this is important?

## What Is a System?

Developing or using systems to help you get things done can unlock a world of creativity, productivity, or even just an ability that you don't naturally have.

A system is a set of procedures or methods that help one accomplish something. That's an easy enough definition, one that allows you to recognize that you use several systems every day. Not all of them are great and not all of them work for your purposes, but you follow plenty of systems. You also likely ignore or don't have systems for certain parts of your life, as well—right? Our goal is to think about some systems that might help you out. And yet . . .

Does some part of you bristle when you think of the concept of "systems?" Do you go into *Braveheart* mode and paint your face blue and shout, "You can take our hours, but you can't take my free time!" or something like that?

Lots of times we react to the concept of creating systems with a kind of chaffing—something that is *especially* true of creative types. I know that's what happens to me; I get a bit twitchy about the notion of systems.

And yet, if you work on the discipline of committing to systems, your life will work a lot better. Your business will work better. It just comes down to knowing *when* to build a system, *what type* of system will work for you, and *how* to keep yourself poking back into the system you create.

## Systems Don't Exist Because You're Weak

In fact, the opposite is true. Famous cellist Yo-Yo Ma was once asked why he still practices three hours a day if he's the best cellist in the world. As you might imagine, he replied that he's the best cellist in the world *because* he practices three hours a day.

A book worth checking out is Atul Gawande's *The Checklist Manifesto*. You can also search for the *New Yorker* article that is a shorter version of what eventually became the book. Something as simple as a checklist can really change your life and improve your ability to deliver.

## When Should You Use a System?

Let's first cover the easiest reasons to use a system:

- **When something is repetitive, boring, and not of high value.** Bill paying is the least fun thing I can think of doing—and it also happens to be something I'm really bad at. I forget to do it all the time, even if I have the money. But almost every bank in the world has online bill-paying technology now. If you're not using it—well, why aren't you?
- **When something needs care and attention, but a little less creativity.** For instance, I seem to want to forget my passport whenever I travel lately. I even have dreams of this now. So now, every time I go to leave the house, I have a checklist (which is a system) to remind myself of the things I tend to forget (another item is international power-converter plugs).
- **When you'd like to conserve all your wonderful creative juices for one part of the project, and not waste them remembering**

details that you could easily plug into a system. Why fill your mind with things that require your active memory that don't contribute to your overall success? When I park my car at the airport, I take a photo of where I parked. Then when I return from a trip, I won't have to wonder, "Where did I leave that pesky car?" and instead, I can worry about how to say, "Your ATM just ate my bank card!" in Turkish (true story!).

- **When you are practicing something and need a system to keep it all in place.** And this can be anything. I'm "practicing" drinking 256 ounces of water a day. That's two gallons. I have a little checkbox in the corner of a notebook that lets me count down in 40-ounce measurements how much water I've taken in. Without that system, I won't keep the pattern moving.

My friend Ron Hood works with Rob and me, and his title is Special Projects Coordinator. He does a lot of things, and all of them are nitpicky and systems-based, and completely out of my league to repeat.

When I went over to Ron's house one day, he showed me all his systems for keeping track of my company. He had binder after binder of real paper, and tabs, and color-coordinated something-or-others. It was unreal. But it goes way beyond this. So I decided to interview Ron to talk to him about what systems do for him, and how he uses them.

## Interview with Ron Hood about Systems

When I asked how all his systems began, Ron said:

It's all related to [a question I ask myself]: "what would happen if I was on my way home from work and I didn't return to work the next day? I would not want the company I'm working for to think, "Oh, my gosh! I have no idea what to do." I'm very systems-oriented, because I want someone to be able to come in and pick up right where I left off.

If I come join a company and there isn't a "manual of everything" already, I create one. If I have to do anything more than a couple of times, I have got to create a system for it.

It's about being efficient, and pulling it all through. When I speak to people that are dealing with you, and I send them a template, I build it all from there so that everybody knows where they are, everybody knows what to expect, and we go from there.

Ron also has the not-very-fun task of fixing every mistake that other people have ever committed with regard to interactions with us. If they mess up, Ron builds a new system to prevent that kind of error from happening again. When I asked him if that made the process too heavy, he said,

I don't see it as heavy. I just think of it as my mind-set. I try to keep my mind open as to how often this is happening. I might say to myself, "This is something I've gotta watch out for." There've been many times when I've worked with people who ask me, "Can I use what you've sent me?"

People take and adapt Ron's way of doing things quite often. I asked Ron why he doesn't just "do things" and not create systems (I'm more of a "let's just do this and get it over with" guy), but Ron insists on systems. I wanted to know: why can't he just "go with the flow?"

I can't. It's my make-up. Prior to getting a system in place, I am flying out in the wind. I'm a bit crazy. I need to get a handle on this—to take pieces and build something from it.

I also asked him—does technology help?

I love trying new technologies to see what will work for us. I love InfusionSoft (our CRM and e-mail service provider). I like all the different technology and finding new uses. Everything can integrate better, and I can find new uses along the way.

There was a lot more to the interview, and you can see it at http://ownermag.com/ronhood. You might find it really useful. And I should point out that Ron is one of the sweetest guys alive; in fact, you'll hear him talk about adding most of our clients to his personal Christmas card list. Oh, and you'll learn just which kind of freak Ron is (the best kind!).

But back to you. Let's talk about you and systems.

## What Type of System Works Best for You?

How should I know? You're you. This is where people get really hung up—and there's no need for it. If you like paper, work with paper. If you love little three-by-five index cards, and crossing off lists, then *that's* a great system for you. Don't think you need the latest smartphone and a tablet and some kind of cloud-centric application—unless you do.

Create the systems you need and use them the way you need to use them. Never ever let the world dictate how you do something. Do keep your mind open to the fact that someone might have a better way to do something; but don't feel the need to always be looking for what's "next" or "better."

At Human Business Works, we use a lot of clever automation technology to help remove repetitive tasks at my company. For instance, people tend to ask some pretty repetitive questions via e-mail, so we have software that lets us type a few characters, and pow! Out come several paragraphs of preloaded information. We then customize it as much as need be for the person's question, and we've saved ourselves many minutes of performing the same process over and over.

Of course, this requires that one use a piece of software like that; in my case, it's called TextExpander for Mac. If you don't use that technology, and instead have a little notepad file with snippets you copy and paste, that'll work, too. It'll just be a bit more time consuming and tedious than the method I just explained. And that's what you need to know about the variation of how systems might work—or not.

## A Very Important Process to Have

Before we go further into systems, it's really, really important to think about this one process: *You must review the systems themselves occasionally.* If you have a system that says "turn off e-mail for six hours at a time so that I can get something done," review whether that's effective once every month or so. (My guess is "yes.") It's always important to know that the system still fits your efforts.

Now, let's lay out some systems to consider.

# My Compass

I came up with this idea when I realized that I was spending (read: wasting) a lot of time doing certain things habitually. I had a system I didn't really intend to have. It worked like this:

- Work on important project. Get stalled briefly or want a break.
- Flip to checking Twitter/Instagram/E-mail/Google+/Facebook.
- Get a drink.
- Walk around.
- Make some calls.
- Get back to the project.

If you can write something like this out, it's pretty obvious you're wasting time. But the problem was that it was happening without me thinking about it. I didn't have a system in place, until I did.

Enter: the compass.

This is simple. I basically have a small note. I keep mine in Evernote, but it would fit on a medium-sized sticky note, too. The note says a handful of things that are important for me. I'll give you a sense of what it says (though not the actual contents; it's private).

**Every morning:** Read compass/meditate/review (the day's work)/ gym/Trello (my project management system)/execute

**Every day:** Fitness/learning/nurture/progress (this reminds me to follow my big goals on a daily basis, instead of in some abstract way).

**Every evening:** Review/plan tomorrow

Let me pause here for a moment. That item that says "plan tomorrow?" Every time I forget or choose not to do that, it screws me. I wasted a *huge* part of today. I had good intentions, but I didn't write anything down. I should have . . . well, "should" is the least useful word in the English language. Who cares? I didn't do it, and my day suffered. Okay, back to compass stuff.

Here are more notes in my compass:

- Take inventory.
- Operate from OODA.
- Boxes and bytes on the map.
- No wasted time. Roadblocks mean shifts.
- Obstacles are temporary.
- Work the plan.
- If there's no plan, make the plan.
- Nothing is a dead end. Leverage everything.
- Grow. Get to the bigger level. Learn.
- Nurture daily. Isolation is death

Okay, I'll be open. All this is what's actually written on my personal compass, at least right now. Beyond that, I won't share. It's more of my own personal affirmations. One of them says "I'm Batman." Yours will differ. Take, for instance, the "Operate from OODA" bullet above, which is:

**Observe:** See the situation that's happening or that needs your attention.
**Orient:** Determine what your position is with regard to this situation.
**Decide:** Decide what course of action you will take.
**Act:** Take the action.

The reason it's called the OODA loop is that it's about repeating this quick set of actions until you've found success. It was determined that the OODA loop was the most successful of several military strategies because it was the most fluid and flexible for the most situations. That simple structure of looping until you succeed made it easier to win.

## Make Your Own Compass

Write down maybe five to seven reminders that you need to focus on daily. And I don't mean that you should think, "Hey, I'll do this later." I mean *stop what you're doing* and make a compass right now.

Be really specific about your needs, but not specific the way a to-do list gives you an *exact chore* for the day—because this is not the same thing. This is a way to keep you tied to your goals and help you remember to dig out of the areas where you might get a bit stuck. For instance, my reminder states, "Work the plan. If there's no plan, make the plan." That would have saved me today. I didn't see it in the compass—or rather, I kind of breezed through my compass this morning. That reminder would have helped me.

Now, make sure to keep your compass somewhere that you can read it daily. I don't care if that means making a few copies; that's totally fine. And don't forget, my compass has three sections:

1. Daily actions.
2. Reminders.
3. Affirmations.

Your compass can have those sections, too, if it helps.

## Some of My Other Systems

One part of my time management and priority management is based on Work Like You're on Vacation (WLOV) (http://hbway.com/wlov). Rob Hatch created this course when he realized that he somehow got a lot of work done in a very little bit of time when he found himself working while also spending time with his family. This has happened to many of us at one point or another. We go on vacation and find ourselves doing some work chores, and earning the evil eye from our family members as a result. Well, Rob found a way to fix it.

What came out of it, WLOV, is a notion about how you can structure your day with systems. It allows you to work really hard for four hours, and then have the rest of the day to do everything else you want to do. Of course, this approach works best when you have control over planning your day. It teaches one how to eliminate distractions, how to prioritize, and so on, and it's a system that I use so that I can be very productive.

Another system I use a lot is called *time quilting*. It incorporates the notion of what a quilt is—a blanket made from scraps of fabric that are no longer useful in another form. For instance, in the old days, a quilt might be made from bedclothes that had holes in them, and a pillowcase that had a stain on one part, and so on. You'd cut out the parts of the fabric that were still good, stitch them together, put some kind of backing on them, and pow—suddenly, you created more use out of material that you would have otherwise thrown away.

Have you ever had to sit in a waiting room? There's usually a choice: You can read magazines from a year ago, or you can work on something you need to do for your business. Find yourself with an extra 10 minutes while waiting for a meeting to begin? Use that time.

I use Evernote for this. For instance, if I'm working on a project that might have to be accomplished over many sessions, I'll keep "next actions" listed in Evernote and work on them a little bit at a time. If I'm writing something (like this book), I'll steal snippets of time from downtime that otherwise wouldn't be used.

Voilà. I have more time than you because I time quilt.

## Three Systems So Far and Counting

I've got the Compass.
I've got Work Like You're on Vacation (WLOV).
I've got time quilting.

See how these can work for you and your freak mind-set? You can be who you want to be because all of these systems afford you the ability to work differently.

Add to this mortgage math, which we first discussed in Chapter 6, and automated updates and reminders. Add to this whatever systems you really want to add for your business. And you'll see what matters.

## Something Else Ron Hood Taught Me

Ron Hood pointed out something really important during my interview with him: sometimes, your system isn't good for someone else. If you're an employeepreneur but also serving a client, never forget that what works best for you isn't always the same as what's important to your end client or customer. Ron said that there were a few instances when he had a system of doing something that was really the way *he'd* prefer to do it, but that it ran counter to how I (that is, his boss) wanted to see the information. So, though he had a way he wanted something done, he found himself having to adapt and make the system serve me.

This is an important reminder: our systems are *ours*, which we create for *our* use. But we have to be sure that they integrate reasonably well with the others we serve, or they might not prove as useful. This might seem to contradict the chapter's title, where I recommended that these systems work for you. But it's the concept of an *interface* that's necessary.

## Interfaces and Translations

Part of the time I was working in the telecommunications industry was spent working with somewhat complex software. Without boring you to death, our role was to help one big telephone company system do something it wasn't built to do by taking its method of issuing a command, doing work on our platform when we saw that command, and then sending back a command that it would understand again so that everything worked. The sequence went roughly like this:

[Blue]—talks to [Red] in its [Blue] language—which tells [Red] to do some things in [Red] language, and then turn the results back to [Blue] language again so that [Blue] knows what to do next.

Wow, I almost fell asleep writing that. But did you get the point?

What sometimes has to happen—and what some freaks do quite poorly—speak only [Red] and have a horrible time helping the [Blue] people/systems/platform understand them. The trick, and it's an important one, is that sometimes you have to translate things for the other people you interact with *into their way of thinking about it and talking about it* so that they know what to do next and so that you can proceed.

Let me give you an example of how this happens in my business. Customer service, public relations, marketing, and sales should all be interconnected, since they all focus on the same thing: the customer/buyer. However, in nearly every company that's bigger than a few people, these departments are little islands with completely different languages, mind-sets, goals, and so forth. Few organizations have any kind of internal communications path between them. So sometimes I will recommend a project that crosses several organizational boundaries. If I don't do the extra step of translating exactly what I mean and how I mean it, the project will go absolutely nowhere.

## The Biggest Challenge with Systems

I saved the hardest part to talk about for last: The biggest challenge with systems is that you have to *use them* and *stick with them*. You have to do what you say you intend to do with them. If you don't, they won't work.

I've found that there are ways to make it easier to stick to your systems, so I have shared some of them, in case you find yourself having the same trouble as me. Good?

# 9

# Are You a Solo or Small Business Owner?

**A**s with Chapter 7, if you're not running a solo business or not a small business owner, feel free to skip this chapter. If you're just curious, then I won't stop you. Read on, superstar.

## The Solo Business Owner Origin Story

There are a few ways that freaks end up running their own business. Maybe your story is like one of these scenarios.

- You got sick of your day job, so you quit and launched your own project.
- Your work was outsourced, so you started something.
- You had a day job, launched a side project, and quit the day job once you made enough money to feel stable.
- Somehow you accidentally started a business.

All of these are possible. Maybe you had a variation of the above. And if not, how'd you get into this mess?

My own story has a few shifts. I left my telecom job and started working with entrepreneur Jeff Pulver. A year after we started, things didn't quite work out; we were too soon to the market. I then moved to working with Stephen and Nick Saber at CrossTech (now The Pulse Network). While there, I launched my own group, New Marketing Labs, as a division of their company. Not too long after, I started Human Business Works as my own stand-alone business. Somewhere along the way, I sold New Marketing Labs into the larger Pulse Network operation, and ran HBW full time.

What's great about how I did what I did was that there was always a salary built into it all. This allowed me to earn money and helped me understand how to compensate employees, and taught me a lot about how businesses are run. By the time I was handling my own salary based on what I did or didn't do, I had a sense of how to generate sales—and I knew that the more I worked on matters, the better it would all get.

It's important to recognize what your origin story is, reflect on it, learn from it, and, when necessary, rewrite it. What got you into business? Is it what you really want to be doing? If not, what is it you want to be doing and how do you get there?

## Should You Work for the Big Guy? Why Are You Solo or Small?

Over the years, many people have told me why it is better to work for a big company. Other times, I've spoken with people who work at huge companies who would rather run their own small businesses. Sometimes it seems as though we're all cats stuck on the wrong side of the door. And speaking of animal analogies, a friend of mine, Damian Arrondo, once told me "Better to be the head of the rat than the tail of the lion."

His point: Being just a cog in a machine is far less interesting than being the head of something smaller. It's a sentiment I've turned over in my mind many times. In my role as an employee, I was part of a small team at a wireless telecom and we had a lot of great flexibility that our clients, larger telecom carriers, did not.

My work as a consultant and speaker over the years has given me the opportunity to work with many large companies, like Coca-Cola,

Pepsico, Disney, Google, Microsoft, General Motors, and so on, and I always marvel at how much organizations of this size can accomplish, how far a legacy can spread, and how many people could really be brought to bear on a task. It's amazing how much leverage a big company can wield—and how big companies can sometimes effect change for the better.

I also know that it takes a lot of work to make anything happen in large organizations. One large company I was working with took 11 months to launch what I thought would be a very simple project. Other times, I was told that while an idea sounded great, it was just too difficult to turn everyone around as quickly as my plan required. So there's that.

Also, as an employee, it can sometimes feel a bit like you're lost in the jungle, a cog in the machine. There are times when you might find yourself railing against the systems and processes that are required to make a big company run.

In reality, there's no one right answer. I have friends who love working for the big guy. It's just not going to happen for me; I can't do it. I'd rather be the head of the rat. Left to my own devices, I'd rather captain the pirate ship than be part of the fleet. The fleet has its advantages, but I always find that having the ability to maneuver quickly is most important to me. I'll take that over firepower.

## Solo and Small Isn't a Placeholder

Some people consider their small company something they started out of a need rather than by choice. While I never want to judge other people's choices, this seems like an unfortunate mind-set. When you choose to run a solo or small business, you make a decision to create something that is helpful, flexible, and fits the needs of the company (even if the company is just you) and your clients.

Running Human Business Works has afforded me the opportunity to pivot the company's goals to match my community's needs. It's also allowed me to run a very simple, not-too-many-moving-parts company that doesn't pour money into overhead for no reason. The three (including me) employees of the business are able to work mostly from the comfort of our homes (or the airport, where I happen to be writing this part for you). And we are able to be very flexible in how we execute our business. Very little of that would be true if the company were big. For me, having a small business has been a choice, and one I gladly embrace.

# How to Be a Freak and Still Be an Owner

This first part is almost embarrassing to explain—but I've met a lot of "business owners" who misunderstand the concept of "business." The basic idea of any business is that you provide some service or create some product that you sell to someone else for an item of equal value, usually money. If you're not making money to do what you do, it might be a hobby. If you're thinking that someone might pay you to be weird, there are precious few opportunities for that to be true.

So, remember that you're in business to serve others, and that those others are looking for a product or service and you are looking for money (or value).

## Build Your Core Compass

When I asked about your origin story, I made the point that working for yourself or owning a small business is a choice—not a place-holder. Again—your job as an owner is to serve others with your product or service. This chapter's underlying message is that a lot of what it takes to be yourself and to be an owner comes down to your *mind-set*—and how you use your thoughts to influence your time and efforts.

Said another way, if you build a compass that "centers" all your goals and interests, it is a great way to help yourself be the owner/freak you want to be. This will allow you to work from a core set of actions based on your beliefs. I promise this isn't "fluffy"; it's how you can do business *your* way. Let's walk through it.

Answer the following questions in this table. If you're sure how to answer, look below and I'll provide some more notes:

| My Question | Your Answer |
| --- | --- |
| What's your core business output? | |
| Who buys this? | |
| Most important task daily: | |
| What's your financial goal per month? | |
| What's the plan? | |
| What should you stop doing? | |
| Where do you find your buyers? | |

These are the questions you have to answer. If you're unsure about what I mean about any of them, here's a bit more detail:

- **What's your core business output?** Basically, *what do you sell*? If you can't say this within a very few words, it may serve you best to redefine and reassess your business. As for me, I produce media and education. That's my business.
- **Who buys this?** If you don't keep your primary buyer top of mind every day, it becomes harder to remember that you're building a business *meant to serve them*. This is most often where a disconnect happens that can be detrimental to your business. Who is the person who buys your product? What you do here matters a great deal to your ability to run a successful business.
- **Most important task daily.** Boy, we can really waste time, can't we? Ask any author what they accomplish when their book is due. There's always a bunch of tasks that fall onto our plate that are specific to the matters at hand, or stuff that's happening in the moment—but these tend to move our most important task out of our thoughts for the day. So instead, write it down in this Compass Planning System. Write down that your most important task to do daily is to call existing customers

and check in, or create more art, or double-check your inventory levels. Whatever it is, there's one task you have to do every single day that you usually fail to accomplish. This is your reminder.

- **What's your financial goal per month?** I don't *really* have to explain this, right? If you're a freak destined to inherit the earth, you need to know your mortgage math at the very minimum (I cover this in a little more detail further on). How much do you have to make in a given month to succeed? That's a great way to keep yourself focused on the fact that this is business that requires revenue. *Know this number*, and work toward it in all you do. Don't obsess, but whatever is the slightly less obsessed thing—do that.

- **What's the plan?** It's amazing how we let the complexity of our world get in the middle of doing what's simple and important. My plan for *Owner* magazine is to grow subscribers and sell business partnerships. It's people and revenue. So my plan is simple to remember, though how I execute it is complex. Yours should be similar. And you don't have to list everything, if you don't want. I've given you a very small list to fill in. Maybe you can just provide the plan to get from where you are to what's next in line. Make sense?

- **What should you stop doing?** To have a list of things you should stop doing is as important as having a list of what you should be doing. For instance, while writing this page, I kept peeking at Twitter, because "maybe something amazing has happened." Guess what? *Nothing* on Twitter is important to my book right now. I don't need to be there. On my sheet for right now? "Stop checking social." I have scheduled times to check in. Stick to the plan. What should you stop doing?

- **Where do you find your buyers?** This reminds you to sell. Don't cringe. If you're not selling, you can't make a living. When I stopped speaking at conferences as often as I had been, my sales fell in the toilet. You miss this detail and you'll feel the pain. Where are the people who want to celebrate your work with you and who pay to have you improve their lives?

Once you fill out a core compass—and bear in mind that some of the information can change over time—you'll have a much better chance of keeping what's important in front of you. I keep mine written into an Evernote file on my phone and laptops. It makes a significant difference in how I do what I do.

## What Is Your Mortgage Math?

A lot of us have a strange disconnect between the concepts of working and making money and understanding what it all means to us and our businesses. Partly, it comes from the disconnect we feel when we're employees. Your salary seems to come from one place and the company's revenue comes from somewhere else—in our heads, at least. Of course, it's all tied together.

When you start out in business, and for the first few years you are in business, it is critical to understand how much money you need to make so that you can make good choices as they relate to revenue. My method was to create something simple called "mortgage math," as I mentioned in Chapter 6.

This is simple on its face: How much money do you need to cover your bills and/or monthly expenses? Here are some examples:

| | |
|---|---|
| Mortgage or rent: | $1,500 a month |
| Utilities: | $500 a month |
| Food: | $1,000 a month |
| Gas: | $250 a month |
| Clothes: | $250 a month |
| Entertainment: | $500 a month |

So, the calculator says this equals $4,000 a month. There you have it. That's what you have to make to cover everything. Compare this to what you're selling, how often you're selling it, and for how much.

Let's list what you sell, pretending you're a web designer:

- Website designs: $2,000
- Website reviews: $200
- e-Book: $10

It'd be great if you could sell two site designs a month, because that covers the mortgage math quite nicely. But maybe that's harder to do. In this example there are three different products being sold, so while the largest ticket items are more difficult to secure, the products with the lower price points will be easier to sell.

Moreover, this business model also serves as a simple marketing strategy, in three steps.

1. Sell an e-book that educates, but perhaps also offers a coupon for a website review.
2. Sell a website review that informs someone which actions to take next, and offer a coupon for a website design.
3. Sell a website design project.

But you have to cover the mortgage math. What will you do to make the numbers make sense? Here are a couple of thoughts.

1. Push really hard on e-books and website reviews and aim for at least one site design project a month. That'd be something like 100 e-books ($\times$ \$10 = \$1,000), plus five website reviews ($\times$ \$200 = \$,1000), and one website design project at \$2,000 to meet your budget.
2. Create a midpriced offer, maybe around \$500, and see if you can get more of those sales.

## Use Mortgage Math as a Time Planner

In my own business, I've used the concept of mortgage math as a way to decide where to spend my time or not. For instance, I once had something I thought *seemed* like a perfect idea. I just knew this was the next big thing for my company. Then I thought about it in more detail and realized that it would involve about 20 hours of work a week—but would generate only one or two months' mortgage, max. And that wasn't good enough.

One method is to keep this question in mind: Will this effort earn me enough to be worth it? If not, then you have to ask why you're giving it your time. However, you also have to be aware that sometimes, something that's low dollar is also a lead generator—or might end up functioning that way. It's a balance—and your efforts have to incorporate that, as well. It's not exactly cut and dried; and yet adding this to your plans will likely help you make some better decisions.

# Working with Other People: Should I?

Solo professionals often come to a point when they realize that they have more work than they can handle. Suddenly, the question of whether to take on a business partner or work with someone else in any capacity rears its head. How do you decide? How do you know?

The moment you bring another person into your business, you have to decide how you'll structure the relationship. Is this a partnership? Is this person a peer or a subordinate? Are you hiring an employee or are you bringing in someone else who intends to have ownership?

If they are to be a partner, that means they get a vote on the business's direction, and maybe on your activities. If they are to be a subordinate, they will have expectations regarding what you are to deliver to them in exchange for their time and efforts. In either case, it means your monthly nut just went up; you'll need to cover another salary and in many cases, other expenses such as health care.

Remember that there are many ways to work with people. You can build a small referral network, an alliance of sorts. You can hire someone on a contracted basis. You can cut back on workload so that you handle it solo. There are many choices here. Don't rush into anything.

## When Partnerships Go Awry

I've known plenty of solo or small business owners who enter into partnerships that fall apart. More times than not, they crumble because one of the partners isn't pulling his or her weight. Or at least that's what the problem appears to be. What *really* went wrong is that there wasn't enough alignment *at the beginning*.

Maybe you didn't set the right expectations or concrete enough goals. Maybe you didn't talk through ways you both would participate to move the organization toward success. Maybe a little guidance for partnerships would have been helpful. Here are some thoughts on what would go into that discussion:

- What exactly are we bringing to the partnership?
- Who is responsible for bringing in sales?
- What happens with sales revenue? Do we get a percentage for being the one who brings in the sale?
- Who services the account?
- Whose vote is final in the partnership?
- What are our agreements about marketing and lead generation?
- How do we handle off-time?
- How do we manage revenue?
- How do we manage profits?
- What type of corporation and/or other legal documents do we need?
- What would we need to do to dissolve this?
- What will we do upon agreement to dissolve?
- What if we don't actually agree on dissolving the company?
- What happens with any outstanding debt if we dissolve?

And so on. This list isn't absolute, and in some cases, there might be a few more questions on here than necessary. But most often, people tend to skip asking the difficult questions at the beginning. This forces them to deal with it during a tense or horrible time. Believe me—I've had hundreds of conversations with owners like you. And I've found that questions like the ones above are what people *didn't* bother to ask before some great friendships exploded into miserable brawls—with no real winners at the end.

## Partnerships and the Future

There's another point to consider when you build a partnership, and that's *what happens if you're successful?* Seems like a strange question to ask, right? We worry a lot when building a business that it might fall apart or that times will always be tough. But have you ever planned for things to go *amazingly well*?

When there are only a few people in a company, everyone has to hold *every* role, more often than not. Everyone is in customer support. Everyone is in sales. And so on. But what happens to the roles you started with when you get larger and have more people working on the team? Where do you develop?

The approaches and systems that worked with partnerships or a small company of three employees might not work as well when you hit 20 employees. And further, there's that really important question of whether you're building a lifestyle business or something a little more sophisticated. This changes how you work with people as well—especially if one of you is quite content in a lifestyle mode and the other wants to grow the next IBM or FedEx out of meager beginnings. As with the other conversation, none of these comments or thoughts or conversations have "right" answers. But if you're not in alignment with your team, you'll get to a point where it won't be pleasant. This is something you want to consider *before* you reach that spot in the story.

# When Your Business Hits the Wall

It dawned on me while writing this book that it's very rare that people write about what to do when your big dream business craps out, or fails, or hits a roadblock. Most books are filled with optimism and happy puppies, and boy, you really are going to have an amazing ride, Buttercup. But that's really not how business goes, at least not all the time.

I'll tell you a very poorly kept secret.

Lots and lots and lots of businesses fail. Many businesses (let's just say all of them) run into hard times at some point. And yet, oddly, very few people like to talk about what went wrong, how to get through it, and what to do next. Weird, if you ask me, that these failure aren't discussed more. After all, don't we want others to learn from our mistakes?

Let's make a quick framework (you know by now that I love these) for working through a bad situation. In this framework, we'll go with *assess and act* as our method.

There are in eight steps:

1. Accept that something's not right.
2. Quantify *specifically* what's not right.
3. Review the plan you're working from. (Not working from a plan? This is the root of everything that has gone wrong.)
4. Recommit to the plan.
5. Set a tighter check-in timetable, for at least three weeks.
6. Review the new data.
7. If everything's good, carry on. Crisis averted.
8. If everything isn't working, review steps one through six again, and consider a new plan.

Here's where most people get it wrong: they take a kind of "choose your own adventure" approach.

- **Stop everything and analyze.** You can't *afford* to stop everything. You can analyze, but you have to do it while you're hunting up money.
- **Keep going—but only work harder *without* figuring out the problem.** If the ship is sinking, it doesn't matter how fast you row.
- **Surrender it all and try something completely different.** This *might* be the solution; then again, it might also lead to ruin.

Be smart, be decisive, be bold, and you'll find your way out of most holes.

## Above All Else: Serve Your Buyer

Where companies of all sizes falter repeatedly is that they run afoul of the people they serve. Years ago, Burger King attempted table service. But their customers didn't want table service. Netflix stumbled hard when they split their customer base into two groups—the DVD-ordering people and the digital renters—an approach that was of no benefit to the buyers.

Even as a solo or small business, you must think this way. Ask this question every day when you wake up: "How can I improve the lives of my buyers and community?" Okay, I know. It sounds a bit sweet and lovey-dovey. But it's business with heart. If you do it wrong—if you do it to serve yourself—it'll feel that way to others, and you'll fail. If you do this well, you'll never go hungry.

## Up Next

In the next five chapters (or what I call the Five Freak Flags) I'll give you even more ways to frame some thoughts and actions to improve your chances of success in being the owner that the world deserves.

# 10 Fall in Love with Not Knowing, Redux

I got a great letter the other day out of the blue from a reader named Jenson Lu. He and his sister, Mei Fang, decided to start an online e-commerce men's clothing retail brand called Mincino (http://mincino.com), selling 10 new men's shirt designs per quarter. You know—why not? As Jenson explained in his letter,

> Unlike other people, we are neither geniuses [nor individuals with] big dreams. We are doing it because we are crazy e-shoppers turned small business owners who . . . think that it's fun to offer male shoppers more offerings from a local and layman perspective.
>
> We aren't ambitious; [we] are pretty down to earth . . . we understand that business isn't about the fame or glamour or riches, but what value will we bring to our consumers, and whether the value is what consumers truly want.

Jenson and Mei Fang are aware that they don't know everything they need to know to survive this experience. Yet their attitude is pretty exciting and admirable.

> Despite the challenges that my sister and I faced—and [the fact that there are] definitely more to come in the future, we shall

embrace the storm as two bootstrappers who have nothing to lose but all to gain: experience and "potential revenue," and probably plenty of clothes to wear for the coming year as well!

Jenson was kind enough to let me know that part of what fueled his journey was reading the stories I had shared of other entrepreneurs who didn't exactly know what they intended to do upon starting their businesses, and knew perhaps by sharing this story here Jenson Lu and Mei Fang might just encourage you to launch a business without knowing all the details, either.

## You Have to Know Only Enough to Start

I first introduced R.J. Diaz back in Chapter 1. You'll recall that R.J. launched his own apparel and accessories brand, Industry Portage (http://industryportage.com), to create totes and duffel bags and laptop bags originally targeted toward the construction, engineering, and architecture community. I started our conversation by asking him just how members of the construction industry reacted to the news that he was going to be designing high-end bags. My (albeit stereotyped) mind-set was that these individuals probably wouldn't be all that accepting of such a choice.

> My friends know I have a design background, [so] they weren't surprised. I don't have a background in textiles or fashion design at all, but they know that there's an artistic side to me.
>
> But I still got a strong reaction [from some people who said]: "Why would you ever do that? What do you know about putting a product, making product, doing all of that?"
>
> People in the construction industry gave me sort of a smirk, like, "Okay, that's a nice hobby," and sort of discounted for awhile until I kept up with newsletters and new product designs, and they realized [that it was someone they should] take seriously—and since then have been very, very supportive.

I asked R.J. what the process was like when he jumped in without much knowledge. He said that he was excited, based on the stories he'd read in books like Tim Ferriss's *The 4-Hour Workweek* and others, but what it finally came down to was that he had to start somewhere and try.

Early efforts were difficult. He purchased a lot of prototypes, hired lots of different types of people to try different designs. Along the way, he learned a lot, spent a lot, ate up more and more time and money, but he got a little further along all the time.

But where did he get the time to do all this? R.J. runs a business and has a lot of responsibilities. Here's what he explained.

[I did it during my] lunch time, and lots of nights. I don't need a lot of sleep—four to five hours—maybe fortunately and maybe by necessity to build this brand. I'd wait until my kids went to bed and that's when I'd work on the stuff that I needed to work on that requires sitting down at a computer. Otherwise, I'd be commuting to work back and forth, [carrying] a sketchbook— and I'm [surrounded by sources of inspiration] all the time. I see people with bags and I'm constantly drawing up ideas, and that's mostly where it comes from.

Obviously, having an iPad, iPhone, and various mobile device capabilities make it easy to communicate and stay on top of the social media side of it, as well as communicating [with] vendors and suppliers, and people that are interested carrying my bags, and trying to arrange interviews with anybody, really, that will listen.

It's one thing to be able to put together a handful of bags and sell them a few at a time over the Internet, but for the brand to grow, R.J. has to sell more and deliver bigger orders, and deliver them on time. I asked about what that process looked like, and what challenges he faced.

My concern isn't so much the sourcing. I have manufacturers, production houses, workshops available to handle pretty much any size order. The bigger challenge is *financing it*. In retail—I'm sure this isn't news to many people—but you don't see a lot of the money that comes in for your product until well after you've produced it.

So the challenge [when you're dealing with] something bootstrapped like this is laying out the cash, and trying not to take on investors. I'm trying to do [that], and not take any outside money. So that's definitely the biggest challenge. Producing a quantity of 10—[really], anything up to 100—is not a problem. [At this point, I'm concentrating on getting] into the fashion seasonal aspect of it.

When I do get the interest from retailers wanting to carry my designs and wanting to carry it in four different color variations, then I'll have to start figuring out how to finance it. I'll also need to start looking at the calendar—at not just the next six months but the next 18 months.

I would love to say that R.J. had a quick answer to solving this, or that I do. But these kinds of challenges are what you face when you decide to make your own way. Should you take outside money? Should you use a funding vehicle like Kickstarter? There are many paths to get where you need to go. But it takes a lot of thinking; it requires that you ask others how they'd approach it, do some hard work, and have a lot of luck in moving to the next level. R.J. will get there—and will acquire some interesting scars in the process. I was asked to take on a very significant project while in the middle of writing this book. I don't know very much about how to do this particular task. I know a lot about the space and the product and the players in the space, but the mechanics of what comes next require that I figure out a lot of stuff in a really short amount of time, with the press and the public watching me while I do it. No pressure there.

But that's one of the ways that you will inherit the life you intend to live and the business that best suits you. You have to fall in love with starting with a blank sheet of paper, with the absolute lack of a useful textbook or model. You have to fall in love with not knowing.

# The Fear of Not Knowing

The fear of not knowing might be one of the most powerful fears of all. It affects many areas of our lives, for sure. When we swim in dark waters, we fear for the creatures that might attack. When we send someone that first big "I love you" or ask someone out on a date, we are filled to the brim with fear until we hear a response—good or bad. The same is true with business, though it often asserts itself far more subtly.

You might say "I can't start my own business. I have no idea how to *run* a business." Or maybe, "I'm only a small shop with two employees. I have no idea what to do to *expand*?" We face many circumstances where we simply don't know what to do—or even what to do next.

How we experience this fear is interesting, and worth thinking about.

* We feel the **baseline fear** of whatever it is we don't know.
* We then **wonder** what exactly we *do* know that's anything like this thing that we don't know.
* If we find nothing, we often shut down at this point and wander into some other task or pursuit.
* Sometimes, it occurs to us to ask someone about it.

It's that third bullet that's the killer. When we decide we don't know enough and just head off into another set of tasks, progress stalls—and we decide we'll probably *never* figure it out.

Of course, this isn't true. It's just a feeling we end up having. If we are to fall in love with not knowing, we have to learn how to find comfort amid the chaos.

# Was It Our Education That Made Us So Afraid?

*Every child is an artist. The problem is how to remain an artist once he grows up.*

—Pablo Picasso

We are taught from a relatively early age that we should know what we want to be when we grow up. It used to be that we had to know by the time we were 16, because those last two years of high school—at least in the United States—would decide our path into college or a vocational education or a job. This is a great deal of pressure to put on a young person—don't you agree?

As I write these words, I'm 43 years old. I had no idea where the road would take me. Can I even pretend to imagine foreseeing anything like where I am now from that point in my life from 27 years ago? No—no one can! And yet, we are pressured as far back as then to know what we want to do with our lives—and to plan accordingly.

College/university is the same challenge made even worse. Imagine spending your parents' money, your company's money, your own money, on something you're not even vaguely sure is for you. Beyond the general courses that prepare us for anything, how will you know you're learning the right stuff?

You just won't.

## The Risk of Specialization

You receive conflicting advice every day. One such piece of advice is this: learn to specialize, but be a generalist. Which one is right? I don't know. What if you learned to specialize in selling via AOL (they used to be a social network)? What if you learned to specialize in artisanal pencil sharpening? (That's actually a service: www.artisanalpencilsharpening.com/.)

The risk of specialization is that it works really well when you can stay with that pursuit. But what if that industry, skill, or approach becomes obsolete? You're faced with a challenge the moment you have to shift into some new field or category.

When I interviewed professional skateboarder Tony Hawk, he told me about the time in his career when he found that he was no longer the hot star in the limelight. He wasn't being paid $10,000 or more a month in endorsements. And Tony had to go to work editing videos. Not skateboarding videos, mind you; it was just work that he needed to do to pay his bills. Does skateboarding translate into any other line of work? Not exactly.

And that's why it's also great that Tony Hawk learned a lot of other skills along the way that he could use to make money and grow even more—until such time as the path to being an even bigger star came about. (I talk about Tony and others a lot more in the last section of the book.)

But there are other challenges along the path to falling in love with not knowing. As freaks, we're quite aware of what it means to see things differently. We're also aware that the world rarely shapes itself to our goals. A lot of us have picked up a really unfortunate fear, though. Are you one of the many who have developed a fear of failure?

## Fear of Failure

I could write an entire book on the fear of failure. Many people have. I don't know how successful those books are, though; because not only do we hate failure so much that we avoid trying, we hate thinking about our *avoidance* of failure, too. We freeze and we look the other way. It's really one of the biggest fears in the universe. Now that sabertooth tigers rarely come to eat us in our caves, failure is the new enemy.

There's more to think about, though.

I tell as many people as will listen the following: My success is built entirely on my ability to fail quickly and then learn and adapt from the results of that failure. If you have a highlighter, this is the best advice I can give you in this whole chapter. Heck, I'll repeat it.

*My success is built entirely on my ability to fail quickly and then learn and adapt from the results of that failure.*

What does this mean? For one thing, by being willing to fail, I can collect data that other people rarely see. For another, this fits with Edison's famous comment: In attempting to invent the lightbulb, he first learned a thousand ways to *not* invent a lightbulb.

Do you know who the most successful salespeople are? They're the ones who hear "no" more often than you, but who make up for it by getting the eventual "yes." This brings up another point about failure;

I'm not saying "work stupid," "deliver poor quality," or "fail in ways that harm other people."

I'm saying that you'll get to your destination faster if you surrender all the emotional baggage that comes with failing (or having an outcome you didn't expect). Ready for some clichés?

- Babies learn to walk by falling down a lot, and then less, and then only rarely.
- An airplane is off course over 90 percent of the time.
- Every successful person you know has far more failures than wins. (Want to see some failed products from Starbucks over the years? http://hbway.com/starbucks).
- Skateboarding tricks are essentially 99 percent failure and 1 percent "I hope someone got that on video."

I could go on, but it's not that kind of book. We're the freaks. We know this. We're used to failing. And now you have a more useful way to think about it.

## A Battle Plan for Failure

If you really want to take on failure, you have to start somewhere. Here are some thoughts on what to do regarding failing:

- **Take small bites first.** If you try to achieve something huge, you have to accept huge consequences in return—you might feel like a bug encountering a windshield.
- **Try not to let your failures impact others.** I had to let go some staff when I wasn't making enough revenue to support them. It wasn't pleasant for anyone.
- **Own your failure** *quickly.* This involves anything from saying "oops!" when you trip while dancing to writing formal apologies

when you can't follow through with a commitment. Not honoring commitments is one of the worst types of failures, but instead of using this as an excuse not to start *anything*, use it as a reminder to commit to others only when you know you can accomplish the task.

- **Learn from your failure.** The only real big bad mistake you can make when failing is failing to learn, too. Study your mistakes. Embrace them. Don't wallow in them. And then move on to the next attempt.
- **Reset mentally after failure.** This one is difficult and requires a lot of practice, but it's a trait all elite athletes know well. If you struck out the last time you were at bat, it means nothing to your next at-bat.
- **Try to fail in new ways each time instead of falling into a pattern.** Sometimes, this is easier said than done. But, for instance, if you always run out of money when building your projects, learn to raise or borrow enough money next time. Then fail in some new way.
- **Remove the words "disappointment" and "disappointed" from your vocabulary.** Never say it about yourself. Ignore it when you hear it from others. The word means, "You didn't follow the script I created for you in my head."

If you intend to fall in love with not knowing, you're going to have to fall in love with failure—because failure is a huge part of that. So let's think about what we need for this "love" to happen.

## What It Takes to Fall in Love with Not Knowing

If you want to start figuring out this puzzle, you need the following list as a framework and a tool set:

- What exactly am I trying to figure out?
- Can I break this project down and list the smaller details?

- Does any of this seem familiar?
- Can I accelerate my learning?
- Can I buy my way past some of this (in the short term)?
- What's a task list that would help me work on this?
- Can I find a similar model?
- Where can I research?
- Who can I call?
- What can a practice plan look like?
- How will I know I'm better?

Let's go through these in more detail. I'll use myself as an example. You should really consider taking a blank page in that Moleskine notebook you bought but have barely used, and following along with questions about one of your own projects.

Recently I've been asked to run a much bigger company than the ones I've founded before. Let's use this as the example.

**What exactly am I trying to figure out?** I don't know what it takes to be the founding president of a technology company, at least not at this scale.

**Can I break this down and list out the smaller details?** I don't know the first thing about how to interact with a CFO. However, it just occurred to me that I used to interact with one at an old job. I don't know how a startup handles managing their human resources issues, but, I have friends in HR. I need to get much better at delegating tasks and trusting a team.

**Does any of this seem familiar?** The wireless telecom company that I worked for employed between 200 and 1,000 people. I was fortunate enough to work with the senior team on a lot of projects, which gave me the chance to witness the interplay of a tech company in the enterprise technology space. This gives me some comfort in knowing about that from my past.

**Can I accelerate my learning?** I can interview people for *Owner* magazine, which will develop great content, but I can also ask a lot of questions that will be helpful to my education. Interviews and consultations are a great way to accelerate.

**Can I buy my way past this (at least in the short term)?** Lots of people tell me they are learning HTML development when they tell me they're working to start an Internet business. Why? Pay someone else $5,000 to build a decent site and get on with your business. Spend your time on the important tasks. Ask yourself: Can I pay to *not* have to learn this? Sometimes, this is a great solution.

**What's a task list that will help me work on this?** If it's not in our daily to-do list, it's not getting done. Mine has a "connect and nurture" task that reminds me to reach out to people important to my business. If I didn't remind myself of that extremely crucial task, I'd get too busy with "work."

**Can I find a similar model?** We all seem to suffer from "no one has ever done this *before*" syndrome—and it's never true. There are models that can help you if you can learn to extrapolate their lessons and think about how they work. The very best advice I have is to look for ideas in different industries and see how you can alter them to serve *your* needs.

**Where can I conduct research?** There's always a way to do a little bit of brushing up and learning. It might not always be online or easy to Google—sometimes it requires a little more research and legwork. Can you find someone who is currently doing what you need to learn? Can you visit some place that helps? What sources do people who are doing what you need to learn trust?

**Who can I call?** Have you ever heard the saying "Your network is your net worth"? It becomes true in a heartbeat the moment you take on a challenge. I called hedge-fund manager and entrepreneur James Altucher because he knows how to negotiate deals. I train with Jacqueline Carly, who also happens to be my girlfriend, because she's brilliant on the topics of fitness and nutrition. Reach out. Who can you call?

**What can a practice plan look like?** Sometimes, what we have to learn requires practice. Similar to the task list, if you're not building in practice, it won't happen. I know lots of people who own dusty guitars.

**How will I know I'm better?** If you don't have goals and potential ways to measure them, how will you know where you are? It's like buying a GPS but never giving it a direction.

## What the Interviewing Process Taught Me: Trying on Roles

Job interviews are strange creatures. You essentially dress in a way that is different from the way that you normally do. You brag in the most humble way possible about your accomplishments. You try to avoid talking about your mistakes. You usually end up saying a lot of things you don't exactly believe, or at least not in the way you're wording them. And you spend time with at least one or two people who really won't impact your job once you get past the gates.

Back when I worked in wireless telecommunications, I was responsible for assembling a team of technologists and engineers to deliver product support as well as software release engineering. I came to learn really quickly that I had to ignore a great deal of what most people consider to be the traditional interviewing process. First off, I didn't care what you wore. It wasn't a fashion show. Second, I knew that if I asked typical questions, I'd get rehearsed answers. Finally, I knew that what really mattered most (to this role, at least) was team cohesion.

If I were to have to build a team again—which I might be doing by the time this book is published!—I would spend a lot more time with role-playing types of questions and scenarios and far less time reviewing someone's paperwork. So ask yourself: Why aren't *you* trying on roles?

Let's say you're someone who loves to bake. There are a few ways you can roll with this, right? You can open up a little bakery (obvious, right?). You can become a supplier to coffee shops or other food vendors. You can build your product for retail consumption (difficult, but not undoable). Or you can sell locally at craft fairs and church bazaars.

These are all roles to consider. They give you a much better sense of how you'll accomplish the goal of taking your passion forward into being a business. But you can go further. If you *do* decide to scale up to retail, what if Starbucks buys your product? They'll need far more than you'll be able to make at your kitchen stove. You'll need to try on the role of commercial cooking space procurer, of trainer, of boss.

Some people just locked up and froze. Thinking this far into the future often fills us with . . . what? Oh right, the fear of not knowing. That's the point—because that's what we have to master.

## Explore Daily

You can really jump-start the process of loving what you don't know by exploring daily. See if you can try something new all the time. Maybe it's just ordering a food off the menu that you've never ordered before. Maybe it's browsing a random page on Wikipedia. Maybe you just sink into someone else's life a little with a phone call (or Skype or whatever) and see what their business is about, and what they are learning.

The concept is simple: Do something you're not already doing. And you don't really have to commit to it or do it deeply. Just try whatever will help keep your brain feeling elastic. If you *do* want to grow and learn from those pursuits, maybe you can issue a challenge.

My trainer and girlfriend Jacqueline Carly, cofounder and editor-in-chief of *BossFit* magazine, created the #12in12 hashtag a year or so ago to promote the idea of learning and sticking with some challenge or commitment every month. If your choice for the #12in12 was to learn some basic conversational Japanese, I suspect your mind would appreciate the stimulation. And along the way, I also imagine you'll find yourself introduced to ways of thinking that will eventually benefit your bigger goals.

## One Important Thing to Know

I've spent the past several pages telling you that not knowing is really cool. I can also tell you that it's essential to know what you *don't want* and what you *don't like*. Though a bit contradictory to loving what you don't know, let me go further into explaining this.

Let's say you decide that what you really want in life is to sell popcorn at local events. It's not that you want to create amazing popcorn; you just want to be a food vendor. Would it benefit you to learn how to run a huge multiemployee business selling popcorn at a hundred locations? Should you go off and figure out how to negotiate with huge corporate popcorn growers?

No, of course not. Not if what you really want to do is sell 20 or so bags of popcorn at the local game and then go home and watch TV.

I worked with a guy who decided he really liked the Caribbean. He wanted to visit there quite often—not exactly live there, but just have more time there than a one-week vacation every now and again. He came up with the idea to sell pirate souvenirs to tourists. He didn't know how to do this, so he researched how to order supplies and how to open a business down there.

But he also knew that he didn't want to live on the islands full time, or run the business himself. He just wanted an excuse to go to the Caribbean on business, thus giving himself a write-off. Because he knew a lot about what he *didn't* want, he worked to accomplish exactly what he *did* want.

You can fall in love with not knowing how to do something—but you should also learn as much as possible about what you *don't* want to do or be or pursue.

## Taking on Too Many Exciting Projects While Not Knowing

While I'm giving out warnings (hey, why not?), I need to point out that a huge deterrent to your future success is the tendency to say yes to too many things. I know—I'm also a *huge* offender of this policy. I say yes way too often. It's something I work on (and fail at) repeatedly. But we have to learn this. It's vital to success.

While I was writing these very words, I was invited to go learn more about making great barbecue from a pit-master himself. Now, I can cook for myself and for not-too-picky people, but I'm not skilled in the mystic arts of American barbecue. Would it be interesting to learn more? Yes. Would it make interesting content for my magazine? Maybe so. Can I spare a day to fly out and experience this? Not really. I'm not exactly dying to jump on planes right now; I've got enough of them scheduled for other pursuits.

I should quickly add that this doesn't mean I won't say yes. I'm a sucker for fascinating "slices of business life" stories.

We can't—and *shouldn't*—learn everything.

Knowing too much seems like a really great goal. When I worked for the wireless telecom, I used to pride myself on being an expert in all of the platforms I worked on. But I learned in short order that this meant people would repeatedly call on me to perform at that level. If I wanted to lead, I'd have to learn how to master the skills of a leader, and let my team become the experts.

It was a really jarring moment. I was used to being proud of my knowledge. But what I didn't realize was that knowing it all was keeping me from knowing what it would take to be successful at *my* game. And this lesson has shown up repeatedly in my learning since then.

When I designed my blog, I used to want to know everything about how to actually install and build the web design. Eventually, I got smart and paid someone who *loved* to design and implement the technology. I now pay a few different people to maintain the technology that fuels my business so that I can focus on the humans whom I serve in that business.

In fact, not only am I very much in love with not knowing, but I enjoy learning less and less about things every day. Instead, I am learning about how to serve the people I support, and we all benefit when I concentrate on this.

# 11 Worship Obstacles and Challenges

*Well, yes. For a few minutes there, it actually occurred to me to wonder what kind of a man would heal a broken child of some of his hurt, just so he could throw him back into battle again. A little private moral dilemma. Please overlook it. I was tired.*

*Saving the world, remember?*

*Call him in.*

*—Ender's Game*, Orson Scott Card

This marks the third time that I've referenced *Ender's Game* in a book that I've written. I consider it to be a very pivotal work in the development of my business success. To that end, I'll summarize it briefly and explain why it's so great.

The story is set in the future, and some alien race is hell-bent on destroying the planet in a major way. Our military forces have determined that the best fighters to win this battle are the most intelligent and creative children.

Ender Wiggin is the boy that the military believes will save the human race; however, they must first educate him quickly in the ways of war. This requires stripping him of any qualities that would make him a "normal" boy to transform him into the weapon they need. This means he can't have friends as you or I would; he has to learn to stand up for himself, because no grownups will be able to protect him in war. And it means that all kinds of obstacles and challenges are thrown at him.

Of course, it's an entertaining page turner—but the book also teaches you to reconsider your perspective. "The enemy's gate is down." (Get a copy at http://hbway.com/ender to see what the heck I'm talking about, and no, the movie's not as good because it can't convey the most important lessons.)

This book also sets the stage to talk about one really powerful habit that freaks need to succeed: the ability to see the same scenario from various perspectives. It's important to see things from different vantage points, to realize that you need to know more than what has worked in the past in order to succeed *now*. It's crucial to learn to rely on your own knowledge, your extrapolation from other examples, and the wisdom of others once you've been put to your own tests. The old saying "What brought you here won't get you there" applies perfectly to this case.

Let's look, for instance, at one shift in thinking you may have to make before inheriting your earth.

## The Corporate Ladder Is Gone

Entrepreneur and author Alexis Ohanian—whom I first introduced in Chapter 3 and whom *Forbes* magazine called the Mayor of the Internet—uses his book, *Without Their Permission*, to highlight the very disruptive ways in which the Internet has changed power structures within both business and politics. When I talked with him specifically about the entertainment industry, here's what Alexis told me:

> We grew up in the middle of all this. We still carry our baggage from a world where TV still has a lot of value for us because we grew up with a handful of nightly news stations that we watched

at six o'clock, or whatever. We have our own biases; I even catch myself. For literally a year and a half, I was pitching my idea to traditional networks, and they all said the same thing: "We love you and we totally want to do a show with you, but it's going to have to be a little different if we're going to sell it to network X or network Y." And then in the end I was like, "You idiot. What are you thinking? Just go on the Internet!"

Ohanian went on to say that at the same time, those who are in power are thwarted by their lack of understanding of the technology at hand.

The biggest challenge that we face is that what seems very obvious to people who understand the technology is not obvious to people who don't understand the technology. And that is the thing that we, and I mean "we" as in all of us who are fighting for the open Internet, deal with. It's a particular thing. There are so many other industries where I think a politician is totally comfortable respecting his or her ignorance. They are willing to concede that they want to learn, they are ready to learn.

Technology is a weird thing; you can see this on the floor of the House during a lot of this open-group stuff. There were people who were so prideful about how ignorant they were about technology, saying, "Oh, I'm not a technology guy, but we've got to pass this bill anyway." It's shocking how boastful they can be. We have to be able to explain this stuff in a concise way that my dad and my girlfriend understand. Those are my two sounding boards, because they are both smart people, but they are not technologists, and if I can explain it in a way that works for them then I'm on the right track.

Everything is shifting in terms of who is in power these days, and the corporate ladder is now the least interesting prospect in a person's career and business ideas—simply because it takes too long. It is bound to a single organization, so you might fall right off the ladder as they're pushing you out the door midway. Do you *really* have to climb every rung?

When the dot-com boom was under way, I was working at my old wireless telecom business. A bunch of our talent left to join startups. They came back about a year later and were all made directors and vice presidents, jumping over everyone who stayed in place. That was my first realization that the ladder was silly.

And even if you *love* your job and intend to be a freak at your cubicle desk (because that's totally part of this ecosystem I'm describing), ask yourself this: would you rather impress your boss or impress the universe? Okay, your boss is the one giving you your annual 1.5 to 3 percent raise. But if you lose your job, the universe will know you're amazing. And by universe, I mean having a perspective on your career as something bigger than the current name in the upper-left corner of your pay check. Do stuff that is amazing beyond the walls of your gig.

## Fear of Failure Rears Its Head Again

One of the most common reasons people cite for not going after something new is that they are *afraid*. I know we discuss this in Chapter 10, but it merits a review here.

As I've been writing this book, it's become apparent that we need more revenue in my own business. Now, technically, *most* businesses need more revenue. But we *really* need a bump or things will start to get uncomfortable very soon. This means we need more sales. Of the three employees I have, I'm the best opener, Rob is the best closer, and Ron is the best servicer of deals that we've closed. But I *had* tried to push off my involvement in sales—because, like most people, I'm afraid of rejection.

Fear is why we don't do things, even if those things are important to us. Making money is pretty critical to my business's survival. So I have to find a way to get around the obstacle of fear and face the challenge: How can I launch new partnerships to gain revenue for my business?

There are three basic ways of dealing with fear.

1. **Yes, and.** You can say, "I'm afraid of hearing *no*." Change this to "I'm afraid of hearing *no*, which might happen, and when I do, I'll try these two extra ideas and see if I can get a *yes*."
2. **That's stupid.** I read in a book on mental toughness that if you pick on your fear, call it stupid, and try to deride it, you might just trigger the counter emotion of "I'm not going to let a stupid and irrational fear get in my way." (I personally find this method difficult, but I haven't practiced it enough to tell you *not* to consider it.)
3. **This is like that.** One way to tackle fear is to trivialize it by finding something analogous to that fear, but lesser in intensity. I've never launched a magazine, but isn't a magazine like a blog with a lot more authors? Look for something to connect with and then come alongside your fear with that in mind.

## So, There's No Ladder. What Is There?

Maybe you run your own art business. If that's the case, there never *was* a ladder. Maybe you took your fine arts degree (or your high school diploma) and started looking for ways to make your sculptures pay the rent. Maybe you didn't want to join some big agency and instead started a solo agency, and maybe you are growing it to where you want to grow it.

Somewhere along the line, a lot of people were trained to believe that there was this neat corporate ladder or simple progressions. But that's not how it works. I'm not sure if that's how it *ever* worked.

What I know for sure is that we *do* have obstacles and challenges. We have puzzles. If my friends who work to make the world better for people living with autism hadn't adopted the puzzle piece as their symbol of choice, I'd take it as the freaks' logo (who knows? Maybe we can share the puzzle piece!).

Why? Because that's what's replaced the ladder, and that's what we all have to deal with nowadays. When you get a few steps ahead in your business, and then your biggest buyer tells you she's moving to a new supplier, that's a puzzle. That's a challenge. That's what owners face.

When you're the blue-haired wizard of your own small empire but not able to pay the bills, you might face the challenge of whether to add on a day job, to find a safe harbor during a stormy time. Is it the freak way to say "Screw this! I'm my own boss," and go live on a park bench somewhere? That's certainly your choice to make (though I'd take the day job, if that's what keeps the kids fed).

We need to recognize and face challenges and obstacles because they are what allow you to shine—and this, frankly, is where your superpowers might surprise the folks who surrendered all their crazy edges so they'd fit in a bit more easily. You will succeed because you'll figure things out where others will wait to be told what to do.

## Rules? What For?

How does a young guy go from airbrushing T-shirts and painting fingernails for girls in New Jersey to running a brand that's made over a billion dollars? He takes on everything as a big challenge. I asked Marc Ecko about what it means to create explosive marketing and build a bombastic brand:

> It's all about distribution. I would challenge that it's going to be hard to satisfy expectations of some kind of great breakout event happening if you're in a too broad distribution channel.
>
> In this day and age, where there's so much static and noise out there, there's also great opportunity if you allow yourself to think a little bit more strategically and in a manner where you might fall down, to try to market in a more specific way.
>
> I think you're a more creatively viable artist if you have a better understanding of your market. Being in the middle of Times Square is an overly broad distribution channel. It's like trying to break in as the new flavor of meat topping at a Walmart superstore.

So instead, you can try to create evidence in places like this, but your job is to be really aware of the commercial aspect of your demographics as well.

In Ecko's experience, he learned that simply being bombastic wasn't enough. It was great for "creating evidence" of value of some kind, but you have to be commercially minded if you want to be a successful artist these days. The myth of the starving artist is simply that: a myth.

His new book, *Unlabel*, has lots more on this. By all means, dig in if this inspires you.

## When Your Big Idea Craps Out

Saul Colt told me a story of when he was still working in the family business of corrugated cardboard. He explains that back then, somewhere in the 1999–2006 time frame, one of his innovative ideas was a little ahead of its time. In this case, Saul decided that the company could really distinguish itself by selling white cardboard boxes. As he tells it:

This was one of the slowest-innovating industries ever, so I believe I can make the claim with almost absolute certainty—we were the first place in North America to carry white boxes. And, now, you think of white boxes as the standard. For example, Apple—everything's white and beautiful. But when we tried to get people to pay two cents more for a prettier box, it almost put the company out of business. I was like, "I'm sure this is going to work." I was maybe 10 years too early, and I almost ruined everything for many, many families; but we were able to dig out of it.

It wasn't an instant thing—because it wasn't like [we] launched something and nobody [bought it and we were] devastated. This was really more along the lines of—we invested a lot of money, filled up a third of our warehouse with a new product, and it would take a little time, but nobody cared at all for this.

"So how did you dig out?" I asked.

It wasn't an instant thing. It took a lot of sleepless nights figuring out how we were going to recoup our money, because it was a major investment. It's one of those things where, if you're building a business of any kind, you have to take small risks, big risks, and calculated risks. If you don't want to be the status quo, if you don't want to just sort of keep opening and closing the door every day and having no change, then you have to take some risks. And some risks work—but some don't. My whole career, everything I've done, I've always been a few years ahead. Sometimes it's worked out amazingly, and this is one instance where it didn't work very well.

And as for lessons learned, Saul has one that will resonate with any attempt you have in any field to be the freak that you deserve to be.

In hindsight, I know exactly why it didn't work: I didn't pay attention to the market. I was pushing my own beliefs on people who really didn't care for it. And you can make all sorts of BS analogies that that's kind of what Apple did and stuff like that; when you're talking about a tech industry or early adopters and people who are constantly just overconsuming whatever's new, that stuff works like a charm.

But when you're talking with 50-year-old guys with mustaches who don't want to change, ever, it's a totally different marketplace. [That's when] I learned how important it is to know the people you're talking to. Take the time to actually learn about your customers. It was one of the best learning experiences of my career, but also one of the most harrowing, because it could have destroyed everything.

I hope none of us are ever in the position to deal with Saul's situation in our own business; but then again, maybe his lessons here will give us a new way to consider it before it happens.

## When the Money Isn't Flowing

When most people think of Tony Hawk's success, they picture his very long career as a professional skateboarder, followed by his role as a businessman managing a very lively brand. We can't always see the bumps that come along the way. I dug into Tony's story a bit and asked him about this exact point.

As things started to decline in the early 1990s I definitely was trying to figure out how to make ends meet. I had a video-editing system that was not state of the art but good enough to start doing sort of freelance editing for people, mostly skate companies. I actually got a few things that were outside of skating through different connections. And [while] that helped pay the bills a bit, it really wasn't enough.

So I ended up selling the house that I was in, moving back into the original house I bought and just cutting back on all my expenses. It was tricky but at the same time, that's the compromise I was willing to make so that I could continue to skate—because I wasn't going to quit.

I really had to jump through some hoops to figure out how to pay the bills. I would get random exhibition offers of skating in a Six Flags parking lot for a week, three times a day for 100 bucks a day. That's the kind of thing I was doing. The only really consistent factor in that was that I just never quit skating. My finances were certainly very volatile. It was crazy. I was going from making upwards of $10–$15,000 a month to scraping to get like $1,000.

In Tony Hawk's experiences are several points to consider:

- **Retrench.** If you're used to making the big bucks but they stop flowing, stop spending big. Cut down on your expenses. Jettison whatever you can to stop the bleeding.
- **Be willing to work.** If Tony had said, "I'm a pro skater. It's below me to edit video to make a buck," he'd have lost it all. Roll up your sleeves and do whatever needs doing.
- **Hold on to the vision.** Tony never stopped skating. Whatever your larger freak vision and goals are, keep those alive, lest you take an endless side road and don't do the work to get back on the path.

# 12 Build Your Own Media Empire

When people ask me how I was able to do everything I wanted to do in business, I tell them that a lot of it had to do with my mind-set—a common theme of the previous chapters. But truth be told, I think the other really big distinction that let me build a business of my own choosing and inherit the earth is that I *created interesting media* that people read and responded to, and that drove business to me. That's the secret sauce.

So what exactly do I mean?

By "media," I mean "information packaged for others' consumption"—blog posts, newsletter posts, an online radio show (podcast), some YouTube videos, and the like. Don't panic. You don't have to dive into everything. You don't have to be a tech genius. You don't *have* to do anything. But again, this is where I stand out from other people whose work is similar to mine.

## Media Lets You Tell a Story

When I write blog posts about certain topics, they get the attention of people who might want more help in that area. I once wrote a post about car dealerships that led to invitations to give keynote addresses for several car dealers' events. The same thing happened with real estate professionals. But that's what this work did to serve me.

I also write lots of posts and create lots of media that's built to help others relate to their own struggles. I wrote a post about self-worth (http://chrisbrogan.com/self-worth) that prompted people to think about their own challenges and to realize that maybe some of what they were feeling didn't have to happen. When you can tell a story that others can relate to, it's pure magic.

But what does this have to do with business? Everything.

## Why Should You Start a Media Project for Your Work?

I have all this other stuff I want to cover here, but I keep thinking, "I wonder if you're even convinced that you should be creating media at all?" There are myriad reasons why creating great media is one of the most important things you will do for your business:

- **Posts on your website will help people find what you sell** via Google and other search engines, and through links on other sites. That's a great reason to post regularly.
- **Creating media is like giving people a free mind-reading power**. They can better understand you, and thus might decide that they want to work with you.
- **Sometimes media help people understand the person behind the project.** If you're in a business where there are lots of similar people, you might find that you have something in common with someone else by sharing stories and interests. I once made a business connection with someone because we both really like Batman. True story.
- **Media-making is a great way to cultivate relationships in between sales.** You can't always poke at someone to buy something. It's nice to have other information to share.
- **It's a new form of marketing and business-making,** and it's a way to make relationships happen that goes beyond the typical "Hey, buy this" kinds of work that came before it.

If I've not yet convinced you how important it is to constantly be generating media, you could choose to skip the rest of this chapter. However, if you're interested in learning more about this, let's dive a little deeper and see what needs doing. Remember, your primary job isn't to make media. That's something you do to *support* your main business—and we can talk about that, too.

## Media Is the Campfire People Can Gather Around

I have this recurring structure concept I want to share with you because it's been the way I've been able to craft the business I've created:

- Content
- Community
- Marketplace

Here's what it means.

Create interesting *content* that people relate to and choose to consume. Use it to build *community* by interacting with the people who consume that content. Be helpful and offer a *marketplace* for services or products that help that community. It's really basic. Want an example?

The UFC is a mixed martial arts league that promotes an entertainment product. Their *content* is a bunch of live and pay-per-view fighting events, a reality show, and related media. Their *community* is composed of aspiring fighters and those who enjoy the sport. Their *marketplace* consists of the sale of some of that media, plus products related to the space. People who are drawn to the media gather, create community, and then spend some of their money, time, and attention on the products and services of the marketplace.

Now, the UFC has only been around 21 years at the time of this writing. Before that, there were smaller and loosely joined groups of people interested in the sport of mixed martial arts—but no one was telling the story in a consistent and unified way. Therefore, the *only* real advantage the UFC had over anyone else was the fact that they told the story better, built a brighter campfire for people to gather around, and then served that community with a marketplace of ways to extract the value they'd created.

## But I Don't Even Know Which Community I Serve!

This is a common response when faced with this task. Maybe you've got no idea what you're meant to be doing or who you're meant to serve. I've certainly shifted my approach a number of times over the past many years. So let's start by making one thing clear: You don't have to etch in stone the names of those whom you intend to serve. You can mix it up. You can adjust. Life will shift with you, and so will business.

I can give you a few hints. Do with these what you will.

- **Serve a community you would serve for free.** The people I like working with most are those who take ownership of their lives, who really want to strive to be the best they can be, and who live to serve others. I love surrounding myself with these people, whether or not there's money in it. That's the best way to know you're in the right place.
- **But if you can, serve a community you might be able to build up and conduct business around.**
- **Always make the concept of community bigger than simply the product or service you provide.** Building a "community for web designers" when you're really trying to sell to "anyone who needs a website" will make it harder to find people to serve.
- **But don't make the community *so large* that people can't recognize themselves.** In the above example, "anyone who needs a website" is probably too large. You might serve the community

you have the most access to reach, for instance. If you were a bartender before this gig, maybe you shrink your media story down to "restaurant business technology," or something.

Again—you might not have the first clue *who* you hope to serve. In that case, there's a slightly different way to go about this. Write about yourself, and be just as personable and transparent as you can be, such that people start to see themselves in your stories. Share your vulnerabilities as well as your strengths. Nothing will get people to relate to you faster than simply being authentic.

## What *Kind* of Media Should I Make?

Let's go through a quick list of some (but not all) types of media you could produce:

- Printed flyers
- Printed newsletters
- Printed newspaper or magazine
- Postcards (often, these are just used for ads, but you *could* make these into more interesting messages)
- Digital blog for posting articles and information
- E-mail newsletter
- Podcast, audio or video sequential and subscription-based information
- Photoblogging, anything from Instagram to Flickr
- Social media, such as Twitter, Facebook, Pinterest, LinkedIn, and beyond
- Video, posted on sites such as YouTube and Vimeo, with content like interviews or how-to.

There are plenty of other media types you could consider. T-shirts could be media. Live events are media. So are billboards. But you get the picture, right?

You have to account for a few variables when deciding what to make:

- **Cost:** Sending paper mailers or renting space on a billboard can be expensive.
- **Time to create:** Producing a web TV show can be very time consuming. On the other hand, a tweet shouldn't take more than a minute.
- **Personality:** Are you great in print, but then stumble when shooting a video? Do you have a "face for radio?" Match the medium to what you're best suited to do.
- **Searchability:** Slightly contradictory to the previous suggestion, but please note that if you don't do *some* kind of textual media like a blog post or newsletter archive, Google won't be able to see you. In the same way, if you aren't publishing to YouTube, you're missing the world's second-largest search engine (yes, people use YouTube to look up information every day).

What's been most successful for me looks like this:

- **Blog:** Great searchability, and a great way to have a home base.
- **E-mail newsletter:** My #1 sales tool. I regret not having an e-mail newsletter sooner in my life.
- **Social network:** Pick whichever you like most, but Twitter has a lot of serendipity, Google+ is a direct line to influencing Google search, and Facebook is often hard to convert into actual business, depending on what kind of work you do.
- A little **YouTube**—again, for search reasons.

Now, you can pick whatever you want. On top of those, I also maintain a podcast (http://hbway.com/radio). Why? Because I read that Mary Meeker from California-based venture capital firm, Kleiner Perkins Caulfield Byers, said that there are 52 unclaimed minutes in the car when people aren't choosing terrestrial radio or satellite. That's almost an hour a day that someone could be willing to listen to your podcast. Is it hard to make a podcast? Not really (http://chrisbrogan .com/podcasting). But that's just how I feel; it might be a lot for you to bite off right now.

## What Are the Stories You Should Tell?

In most cases, you create media by thinking of a story that needs telling. But what do I really mean? Here are some ways to think of what to create:

- **Answer the questions** your community members might have. A lot of the topics I cover in my blog or newsletter are inspired by the questions I am asked when I connect with my audience.
- **Tell your community members' stories** by interviewing or profiling the people who inhabit the space you serve. If you sell skateboard accessories, talk about the people riding them. If you're an artist, talk about galleries and their owners.
- **Tell the "behind the scenes" story of what you do.** Everyone loves to see how something is made, or your process, or something else that isn't typically available simply by purchasing it.
- **Interview the people who deliver the greatness.** I once asked an air-conditioning company what separated them from the other companies. They said it was their team of installers. So, we shot some video interviews with those people, asking them questions about what drove them, what made them work so hard, and so on. The results were a bunch of proud people talking about quality—which is exactly what you'd want to see in any individual you're trusting with your money and time.
- **Tell larger and inspiring stories.** The people at GoPro tell stories of their wearable cameras by sharing the lives of the people using it. Want an example? Watch http://hbway.com/lion and you'll be blown away. (Warning: There are lions and humans in close proximity.)
- **Tell simple and instructional stories on how to do something,** not only with the product or service you sell, but in the space that

your community populates. This is how others succeed many times over. For instance, if you sell video services, you can be like Israel "Izzy" Hyman, who built an entire business around how he does things (http://izzyvideo.com)—one that still gets you paid gigs. Izzy makes videos like "how to light an outdoor wedding video shoot and explains in enough detail for you to do the work yourself. And yet, he makes lots of money consulting and selling deeper educational products, and more. Because people pay attention to Izzy's how-to information, when he's ready to sell, he has a very willing audience.

There are many other ways to create media that will draw your audience in, but these should get your mind going. If you want hundreds of more topic ideas, go to http://hbway.com/bt for blog topics.

## How Should I Tell the Stories?

Ah, this is the most subjective part of the experience. Earlier, I mentioned that you should probably have a blog so that Google can find the words you type and send people your way. I mentioned that a newsletter is the best selling tool I've ever had. I said that YouTube is really gaining strength as a powerful search tool (as well as entertainment hub). But beyond that, a lot of this is entirely up to you.

I once had a CEO tell me she wasn't really great with writing, but she was magnetic on film. So I recommended that she shoot videos, and maybe outsource the writing to someone else. You might not have the luxury to hire a "someone else," but you can always weigh your choices to match your ability to create.

I really enjoy looking at photos on Instagram. Sometimes, a simple photo can tell the story well enough to get people's attention. My friend, Joe Sorge, runs a very successful group of restaurants in Wisconsin (some in Milwaukee and some in Madison, so far), and he uses Instagram to show off what's cooking. You will be hungry if you look at these photos: http://instagram.com/joesorge.

Another friend of mine, Mignon Fogarty, runs the QuickAnd-DirtyTips website and hosts a show called *Grammar Girl*, which is mostly audio: www.quickanddirtytips.com/grammar-girl. A while ago, she asked my advise, because she was feeling some pressure to make videos as well. We both agreed that while she could pull off the move, it was a lot more work than the value returned; so for the most part, Mignon has kept her product an audio show. And that's what works for her.

That's just it: Even though I say "have a blog, do a newsletter, consider some video," it is, of course, ultimately your choice. If I said "you *must* make video" and you really can't stand the way you look on camera, then will you take that advice? Not likely. So, adapt as best as you can. Just realize that every choice might have a consequence. You might notice that I didn't do a lot to recommend making your media in print. While I'm not ruling it out, the number-one challenge here is that print *has up-front costs and commitments*. Yes, some of what you do online costs money, but it's often negligible compared to the expense involved in, for instance, sending out a mailing. *Owner* magazine is digital at ownermag.com because I don't want to pay to print, to ship, to store, and to deal with all the related waste that goes into printing a magazine.

## What Not to Do

I try not to discourage anyone from anything he or she wants to do. But there are some choices that can be fairly detrimental to your business, so it'd be silly of me to let you make errors like these if I can help prevent them.

- **Don't centralize your online presence on one or two social networks and think it's your "home."** Facebook can close you out for a rule violation—and if that's your only online presence, you just lost everything in one shot.
- **Don't pick a social network because "I read that's where everyone is."** For some strange reason, LinkedIn doesn't really

help me grow my business the way it helps other people. I get more from Google+. You have to do what works best for you and your business, which you'll only discover by doing.

- **Don't tell "me" stories.** Don't spread the tales that make you the hero or the champion, that end with people saying through gritted teeth that you are *so* amazing. No one wants to hear these.

In the next section, I suggest what you want to do instead.

## Make Your Buyer the Hero

The best not-so-secret advice I can give you is to make the reader of your stories the actual hero in some form or another. You don't need to write "you" stories, but instead use a name and suggest "people like you," as in the following example. Jared Easley covers a lot of groundwork when he researches his guests for his great podcast, *Starve the Doubts*. His thorough approach of knowing so much about the guest that he asks deeply relevant questions is unparalleled. What ensues is a really worthwhile listening experience; no matter who the guest [is] you will feel grateful to have learned something in the process. Jared's work is exemplary of great media making.

This story is about a person in my community—a real one in this case, and you really *should* check out his podcast, *Starve the Doubts*. The story might get you interested in taking a course I offer on how to conduct better interviews, because you can think to yourself, "Wow, I really hope I can learn to be as good at interviews as Jared."

Or maybe I'm selling podcasting hardware, and I use this story to illustrate a success story right before pointing out that *I* have the tools you might need to improve the likelihood that you will become successful. It's not really important exactly what I'm selling, at least for the point I'm trying to make. My point is that I'm not talking about myself or my dumb product. I'm talking about someone who is representative of you.

The key is, no matter what story you tell, make your buyer the hero.

## The Mirror Approach to Media Making

One other way you can create interesting media for your community is if your very own experience mirrors your prospective buyers'. For instance, let's say I'm selling fitness equipment of some kind—promoting heart-rate monitor watches for Polar. I can show you pictures of me at the gym using the product, and talk about how I incorporate heart-rate variability training into my fitness plan. Thus, I make the story about me, but only as the mirror of what you yourself will face.

I know this seems to fly in the face of my previous rule to not tell *me* stories, but this is different. I'm using "me" as the stand-in for "you." Get it?

Let's say you're trying to build a business around a spa that you've launched—you know, that spa your family said was a crazy idea and that your friends can't believe you've opened. You could do what most people do and send out a flyer with a picture of a woman in a turban lying on a table while a masseuse smears oil on her shoulders. Maybe you'll use some faux-Asian typeface and earthy hues, and maybe there will be graphics that represent one or more of the elements. (I've just described about 85 percent of all marketing material for spas, by the way.)

Or maybe you'll snap a photo of your kids' really cluttered play-room, a photo of your overloaded-with-papers-and-stickies desk, and a photo of yourself with not merely bags under your eyes but full-on *luggage*. And these photos, nicely combined in a three-piece frame, can be shared on your website or Pinterest or wherever, with a simple tagline like "Ever have one of those times?" And maybe there's a link back to your primary site, where you sell white turbans and scented massage oils.

Sometimes, your life is your buyer's life. If that's the case, you might as well promote the business by making yourself the mirror of the buyer you intend to attract.

## The Media Empire Mind-Set to Success as a Freak

When I was growing up, a business had to do one of the following to succeed:

- Convince a newspaper to write a story about you or your company.
- Buy an ad in the paper, on radio, TV, or whatever media you can afford.
- Pay for expensive mailings.
- Convince a big company to carry your product.
- Hope you have lots of great word-of-mouth publicity.

While all those opportunities still exist, there are many more ways to promote and build your business nowadays. Instead of resorting to the conventional gatekeepers, you might:

- Write your own blog post, shoot your own video, or make your own ads.
- Buy ads on Facebook or Google or promote a tweet on Twitter.
- Maintain a vibrant e-mail newsletter and marketing platform.
- Sell your product through online platforms like Kickstarter or Etsy.
- Enhance your word-of-mouth presence with social media.

The best place to start is by building a website of your own, where you might keep a blog of some kind. And remember that "blog" just means a tool for creating and posting content—sometimes in a sequential form—and hopefully offer some way for people to subscribe to receive updates.

From there, you might consider building up your e-mail offerings. And from there, you might choose one or two social networks. I also mentioned the use of YouTube. All this, to my mind, has the makings of your media empire.

Is it hard work? Yes. Is it something you have to do? No. But it can be the *least expensive* way to build and maintain a useful relationship with the community you have the pleasure to serve, and to nurture the marketplace where you can sell your products or services.

We've covered this enough for now. There's a whole book (or 100 books) we could read and/or write to cover more methods, but you're either engaged in developing your media presence or not.

Now, let's see if we can find some more freaks.

# 13
## Connect with Your Freaks

**A** long time ago in a galaxy far, far away, I was a boy growing up in the middle of Maine. Most of the kids in my neighborhood wanted to talk about Van Halen versus Led Zeppelin, Mustang versus Camaro, and the Red Sox versus the Yankees. These were the conversations available to me—which was fine, except that I already knew the answers: Van Halen, Camaro, Sox (but didn't much care about the last one, because the Sox hadn't won a series in over 80 years). These topics just weren't that interesting to me.

I was into Batman and Star Wars and anything weird—whatever my friends and neighbors and relatives *weren't* into. Worse, I was into old stuff like the really classic sci fi that my dad and grandfather introduced me to. And I could talk to my dad about that, but you know, when you're a kid, that doesn't seem like the coolest choice in the universe (although most of us grow up to learn otherwise).

Flash-forward to my high school years, and the family owns its first Macintosh—the boxy one colored like a manila envelope. My dad bought a modem, to connect the computer to other computers. Then he introduced me to bulletin board services (BBSs). I'll presume that most of you don't know about BBS stuff, because it's long before AOL and CompuServ and Prodigy, and long before the Internet as you know it.

Imagine a program that is like Facebook, but only one person can use it at a time (when two or three people-at-a-time BBSs were developed, it was like the *future* had arrived!). So, one person would log on, post something about how Superman was better than Batman, and then they'd log off. I'd then log on, tell that person they were full of crap and didn't know anything and that *clearly* Batman was *way* better than Superman, and I'd log off. The other person would dial back in, call me and my entire family a bunch of stupid inbred monkey pigs, and then hang up. And hooray, primitive flame wars began! (Although, in all fairness, I presume the *real* primitive flame wars involved cavemen and fire.)

What I learned in the long run was that I could talk to people about the things that I was *really interested in* instead of just talking to my neighbors about whatever they felt like talking about.

## You Are Not Alone

One truth that I wish every human alive knew: *You are not alone.* If you are someone who is *really* into creating replicas of Dr. Who characters and settings with glued-together-and-then-painted grains of rice, I promise you, there's someone out there already doing it. Or doing any other crazy things you're pretty sure you are the only one doing.

As I was writing this, I thought, "I wonder what would happen if I just typed something really silly into http://images.google.com." So, I typed in "Batman baby." You should stop reading right now and do this. Go ahead. I'll wait.

Nuts, right?

But this is partly why I wanted to write this book: to assure you that you're not alone. If you've always wanted to be an entrepreneur, create your own type of business, or do things in your own unique way but always felt like everything and everyone around you was telling you that you have to fit in, it's not true. You don't.

## It's Rare to Have People Understand a Freak

Professional skateboarder turned businessman (who still skateboards) Tony Hawk, whom I first write about in Chapter 10, was lucky. He had the rare experience of having parents who understood his passion for skateboarding and who had an inkling that this could be a business for him. I asked Tony about that—quite frankly, expecting a different answer from the one he gave me.

> My parents were very encouraging of my skating. I was lucky; very few of my friends' parents wanted them skating at all.
>
> But my teachers were not so supportive. They thought I was wasting my time taking it so seriously and [were concerned by] the fact that I was not doing other activities. I actually quit [other activities]. I [had been] playing violin pretty actively. I was actually in the school band. I was doing extracurricular concerts as well.
>
> I felt like I had to make a decision: Can I do this or not? And I remember the music teacher being very upset with me and just thought I was wasting everything with my skateboarding.
>
> I also [stopped playing] Little League, and my coaches just thought I was crazy. But I wasn't really enjoying it. I enjoyed violin, I regret ever quitting that, but I didn't regret quitting other sports. I never felt like I was excelling in them. I never felt like I was improving in them at a rate that I could really judge or feel. But every time I went skating I got better at it. So that's why I stuck with it.

The amount of people who will convince you that your idea is wrong usually grows in accordance with how unique the idea is.

If, for instance, you decide that you want to play the ukulele and ask strangers to fund your album and end up giving a well-received TED talk that ends up bringing you to the United Nations to talk about women's issues, then some amount of people are going to think you're off your rocker. Just ask artist, musician, and writer Amanda Palmer. You have to find your freaks, or else it'll be a lot harder to believe that you're on the right track.

Palmer is married to Neil Gaiman, a grand freak in his own right, who creates mysterious and macabre worlds that span comic books to novels to movies to video games to children's books and beyond. My girlfriend and I had the chance to see Palmer and Gaiman read and perform for a friend's book opening in Lexington, Massachusetts, and the crowd they drew was the most wonderful assortment of freaks you'd ever want the pleasure to know. From velour capes to his-and-her matching fishnet stockings to all kinds of sparkle glitter and beyond, it was just the kind of audience that made people feel as though they'd found their tribe. Had I attended this same event when I was, say, 17, I'd have begged Palmer and Gaiman to let me follow them around like an ersatz gypsy.

And perhaps the most exciting part is that everyone in the room understood each other. There was no one in the building who didn't respect and appreciate each other's choices of weirdness. And that's what we're seeking, in many other industries.

And if you're lucky enough to be Tony Hawk and have your parents' support, that's grand. Famed horror writer Stephen King most certainly supports the choices of his famous horror writer son, Joe Hill. And I count myself among the lucky: My parents both appreciate and support me for the freak that I am (and, hey, they ran off to Vegas to play poker and see shows and play host to an international band of misfits—they're freaks and I support them, too!).

And if you don't have that kind of support—well, that's okay, too. But you should find ways to network and connect with fellow freaks—with the people who love what you love and who support what you support. Because that's where you'll find success in your business.

## Remember: "Freak" in Our Definition Just Means "Not How It's Normally Done"

With his wild hair and unbelievably deep-hitting writing, James Altucher is most certainly a freak—but the kind who also ran hedge funds and invested in businesses, and who sits on several corporate boards. He knows more about making complex business deals than anyone I know and yet he's also obsessed with . . . well, lots of things, but one that I know of is online chess. He plays chess any time he's near his computer.

If you feel like you're not the norm and won't ever be the norm, that's our definition of a freak. Now, let's get back to connecting you with your own definition.

## The Bat Signal Effect

Whenever Commissioner Gordon wanted to get in touch with the Caped Crusader in the Batman comics, he wouldn't pick up his iPhone; rather, he'd hope like heck that the crime happened at night and that the sky was full of clouds, and then he'd shine a big spotlight in the sky and signal for Batman.

I used to wonder about this: "How come there was only *one* *superhero* in all of Gotham City? Why wouldn't the bad guys use the Bat Signal to know that it was a great time to commit a crime?" After all, Batman would be hanging out with the Commissioner, right? But I digress.

If you use that media empire we discussed in the previous chapter to reach out and share your interests, you're going to attract the kinds of people who might like what you like.

Marie Forleo speaks to a specific crowd. Her MarieTV and B-School online course has allowed her to speak to exactly the kind of people with whom her message resonates most—primarily, women who want to be the kind of entrepreneur who bleeds passion and lives to cash the check. I asked Marie about her choice to invest in professional video technology to make her video even better. Well, honestly, I accused her of trying to grow up.

> I [don't think I ever actually decided] to be a grownup; [I just concentrated on] having a lot of fun with fancier toys. [I thought], "Oh, we can be even sillier and more ridiculous if we have some more interesting gear." I got to learn how to use things like green screens, where I can be the dork that I am and superimpose myself on videos from the '80s.

That kind of stuff is the motivation for always doing what I do. I'm [constantly asking], "What can we do to make this even sillier?" And sometimes that does require some different gear and kind of going out there and making investments like that.

Clearly, Marie isn't trying to emulate BloombergTV. No offense to the nice people there, but she's looking for the wild and funny and crazy people who still want to be able to put money in the bank. And Marie's business is positively thriving—because people who love who Marie is and what she represents pay to participate in her online community and her other projects. They see the Bat Signal of MarieTV and want to know more. That's the goal.

## Not Everyone Will Love You (But That's the Point)

I asked Marie Forleo about this; after all, not everyone is going to be our fan. I mentioned the fact that there are likely haters out there who don't like her style—and this is what she said:

It's funny how [some] people will just use you to get upset and angry about things. It's incredible what people pick up on in my videos—what [offends them], what they think I'm "evil" for [doing or saying]. It's outrageous. That's one thing you just have to know: If you are brave enough and courageous enough to say, "I have something to say, and I want to say it. And I want to use these modern tools of entrepreneurship to share it with the world," you've got to be ready [for some negative reactions]. Because they are going to come out of the woodwork and say the weirdest, craziest shit to you—and you have to not take it personally.

I have to confess that this lesson was one of the hardest to learn. I used to think/want/believe that everyone had to love me. I believed that beyond reasonable bounds. If someone—*anyone*—had something negative to say to/about me, I'd take it to heart. I'd worry that I wasn't good at my business, that I was wrong—that I was a *bad person*.

It took me a long time to realize that if you're doing something to really reach *your* freaks, then you'll upset someone on the other side of the spectrum who doesn't connect with what you're putting out there. You just have to be ready for this. In fact, often the reality is that *if no one hates what you're doing, you're not doing it right.* (Corollary truth: If *everyone* hates what you're doing, you might want to reconsider.)

## It's All about the *Monchu*

I introduced you to the word *monchu,* an Okinawan word meaning "one family," back in Chapter 5. If you'll recall, it means something like "the family you choose"—and I first learned about it in the documentary film, *Happy*. One scene showed a bunch of wonderful old ladies from a village where everyone lived much longer and under better conditions than most anywhere else in the world. These women went beyond blood ties and connected with each other as if they were family. They thought of each other as sisters, and cared for each other far beyond the borders of being "neighborly."

I love the concept, so I stole it to use for my approach: "Better than networking." You have your family. You have your customers. You have your network. The mind-set of *monchu* is that you care more about some people than as merely customers or part of a network. It's the idea that you're not just looking to make money and "sell and run," but that you might want to build a community *beyond* just selling.

Tony Hawk certainly works from the *monchu* mind-set. One way that he demonstrated this was by creating not only high-end products, but also affordable versions that budget-conscious people who loved the brand and wanted to participate were able to purchase. And he took a lot of heat for this. In his book (which is so very worth buying), *How Did I Get Here?*, Hawk printed both angry letters from people saying that he "sold out" and grateful letters from single moms who were able to buy their child one of the more affordable skateboarding products.

> I set out to make quality, starting beginner skateboards at [somewhat lower] prices . . . [the kind you find at] the mass retailers. Wal-Mart, Target. It was a challenge. I had to fight a lot of battles in order to do that. I fought for better bearings that equate to like 50 cents more a skateboard and the manufacturers that were doing that were telling me, "This board can't be $30! That's crazy." And I'm like, well, why does it have to be $20 or $100? There's got to be some middle ground here.
>
> So we fought for it and we eventually got it. They're definitely not [the boards] professionals use, but they're not going to be boards that kids buy and they're pieces of shit and it discourages them from skating because they're not functional. They're actually functional and they work for especially kids that are starting out at the skate parks and things.
>
> I guess I was the first [member of the skateboarding world] to ever do anything on a mass scale and take that sort of heat of being called a sell-out. And I was willing to do [that], but most[ly] I was willing to do it to grow skateboarding. You know, it wasn't about making money, necessarily. It was more about making it accessible to kids that want to start. And that's the same thing I do with my foundations. Trying to provide facilities for kids that maybe would have never had them and have never had support . . . that they chose skateboarding.

It's interesting that the lesson of building *monchu* connects to the lesson that not everyone's going to agree with you. Hawk faced critics who labeled his move to serve the low-budget marketplace as either selling out or trying to squeeze more money from his fame. Yet his intention could not have been more admirable. He was simply seeking to do what he's sought to do since taking on the mantel of unofficial (and sometimes official) ambassador for skateboarding: get more people involved in the sport.

His Tony Hawk Foundation (tonyhawkfoundation.org) continues to work to grow the skateboarding *monchu* all over the world.

So if you love what you're doing—if you've actually found the community you are privileged to serve, if you seek to help your *monchu* succeed—then you have an opportunity.

But let's say I've convinced you. *How* do you actually do the work of setting up that Bat Signal and reaching out?

## Connect with Your Freaks

There are two ways to attempt to connect to the people you want to reach. One is to try and pitch your best sales efforts at someone you hope to make money from, or you can be open and clear and share *exactly* what you feel with the people you hope to reach and help. And if you want to do the latter, I can do something to help.

Use the media empire you've built. Cover the stories that would matter to the people like you in the community you have the pleasure to serve. And be as open and connected to everyone as you can be. Build your *monchu* by giving more than you ever hope to receive, and in that process, you'll have the ability to improve your opportunity for success.

How do you reach them? Tell stories using that nifty media empire we built. Show how you relate to the community. And reach out to people to tell *their* stories so that you'll all have the opportunity to connect around that powerful campfire of your joint experiences.

There are numerous examples, especially online. If you're into the video game Minecraft, there are several stories and inside jokes and songs that it seems everyone interested in the game all know. For Halloween, my son wore a Creeper costume (one of the characters in the game). The way the kids rushed up to him as if he were a celebrity spoke to the way people who play Minecraft feel when connecting with any of their community. Heck, I had a little Minecraft pin on my jacket. It looked like a bunch of pixellated green and brown squares. The girl at the popcorn counter at the movie theater knew right away what it was, and said "Hey, nice pin!" I was floored.

That's exactly what you want. You want people to feel as though they're part of your tribe. It's the whole experience of knowing you've found the Batman and Star Wars conversations instead of the Zeppelin/Van Halen arguments (5150!).

Once you have a sense of *monchu*, there's a chance at gaining the biggest opportunity of them all. Ownership. Let's go there next.

# 14 Own Everything

I'm quite biased. I run a magazine called *Owner*. The concept is simple: If you want to succeed, choose to own your life, your business, and your future. For you, the goal is to take ownership of your choice to be who you are, and do business in a way that fits your interests, your needs, and the way you feel you connect with the world. So this chapter ends up being about that: ownership, starting with personal ownership, and then moving into how this applies to business. It's about the systems and the mind-set and the choices that it'll take for you to be the freak you want to be.

What we'll cover here doesn't sound immediately like business, but it's 100 percent the work you have to do with yourself to grow your business. Because you, my friend, are the business.

Louis XIV of France once said, "*L'état c'est moi*" ("the state is me" or "I am France"). It was a new way of looking at the nation, because people usually thought of the soil and the flag as France. Louie had his own plans, but let's paraphrase his saying: "The business is you."

## Own Your Words

First and foremost, a lot of what happens in our world comes from words. You talk to yourself all day long (out loud or otherwise).

And if you're really honest, a *lot* of what you say to yourself is more negative than positive, isn't it?

- How many times a day do you call yourself stupid?
- How many times a day do you curse yourself for doing the wrong thing?
- When you forget something, what do you say to yourself next?
- How many times a day do you tell yourself you *can't*?
- Are you the kind of person who says "You're not good enough" to yourself?

I could go on, but if you didn't recognize the voice of your Inner Critic in all this, then you're either the most adjusted person alive or you are lying to yourself. You decide. But we have to take ownership of this, because it becomes apparent in our "outside" voice, as well. How often do you say:

- I suck.
- I'm a loser.
- I'm a failure.
- I'm no good at _____.
- I've always been bad at _____.

It's really crazy, right? The more you look at all the negative self-talk you give, and the more you think through how many times a day you say horrendous things to yourself that you'd never say to another living soul (one hopes), it really starts to make you think. But we can't stop at thinking. Also, this comes out of your mouth, too. Want to see some examples?

Here's a list of phrases that you want to learn to stop saying:

- I should. ("Should" means "won't" with a side-order of guilt.)
- I hope.
- They won't . . .
- Nobody.

- Always/never. This is one of my biggest fallacies. When I'm upset about something, I immediately think "Things always go badly for me" or "People never recognize me for what I know."
- I wish . . . (wishes aren't nearly as useful to you as goals).

How many of these do you say? In fact, looking over *only* the concept of "own your words," if you were to take an honest look at yourself, how much of what I listed resonates with you and how do you feel about that?

Own your words. Your words are the maps to your intentions. They are the triggers to your potential victories and are no doubt the fuses that light your current problems. If I told you that just fixing this inside you would change your life, would you believe me?

Who do you admire? Think about the person. What kind of language do they use around you? How do they act? How often are they out of control or angry or overly emotional? Do they say things positively? Do they word their intentions in a way that you appreciate? I suspect the answer might be yes.

## And Yet, Own the "Bad" Words, Too

I'm Buddhist, and one of the tenets of my particular belief is that there's not really much that can be classified as good or bad. I won't bore you with this old story that goes back and forth between events that you might label "bad" but that end up being "good" because of XYZ. Just understand that I tend not to like judging words.

But if I title this book *Freaks* and if I'm calling you a "freak," then that doesn't sound like it matches with the whole "Own Your Words" concept that I just explained, does it? Here's the caveat.

Words sometimes have the ability to upset us. Labels that others give us can sometimes cause us grief. And your triggers aren't mine and vice versa. Call me a hayseed because I'm from Maine and I could care less. Others would be very angry. Call me immature and I'll bristle (even though I most definitely *am* immature!). But that's ours to own, as well.

## Own Your Intentions

On the morning I wrote these words, my car was stuck in a snowbank. But I had to get to the gym. So I hired my neighbor, Jane, to kindly take me to the gym (she runs a livery service at coopercoach.com). There are no excuses when I have set intentions.

This is the attitude we have to adopt if we are to be owners. You must own your intentions. As you've already learned in your life, there are easy and hard paths to take. The truth is that what we're seeking is somewhere in between, like a balanced pressure.

Every limb of your body operates on this same principle, by the way: Your biceps and triceps help move your arm forward and back. Your quadriceps and hamstrings help move your legs. Without tension from both muscles, you can't move in the desired path.

More often than not, many of us get in this habit (let me know if you spot yourself in this description):

- Set an intention (I will lose 30 pounds by summer).
- Start with great fervor (gym five times a week, salads, etc.).
- Peter out a week or so later (but it's mom's lasagna!).

Intention, drive, collapse. It's a pattern a lot of people follow. It's built into nature and life, by the way. We should look at that for a moment. Indulge me?

The *easiest* state in nature is entropy. That's when things break down, when they just exhaust their energy and collapse. Nature is all about letting things collapse. Because if you give up in nature, you're just making room for something (or someone) else to win.

But all growth in nature comes from pain and stretching past a hardship of some kind. Childbirth is painful. Muscles grow when you tear them apart, and then let them rebuild. The tree that thrives in the forest tears its bark over and over to grow.

And even in nature, intention is what drives this. I'll let philosophers and scientists decide whether trees "think." But we humans?

That's all we do. Far too much. Far too often. Well, if you're going to bother thinking, let's commit to owning your intentions.

# A Secret: Willpower Is Stupid

If you're going to own everything, I have to let you in on one of the most important secrets I've ever discovered: Willpower is stupid. It's a very weak muscle. It's the least useful way to accomplish any goal. Why? Because it's very temporary. It's a bridge, or a short boost, and it has nothing to do with sustained effort. Willpower is all about pushing past a temporary barrier. What you need is intention and vision.

In my own life, I'll tell you three intentions of mine and how they work:

1. **I am a king.** I act kingly at all costs, meaning that I'm polite, poised, and kind, but will go to war for my goals. I also love my family above all else.
2. **I am an athlete.** The moment I decided I was an athlete was the moment I knew that it's easy to eat healthy and go to the gym at 5 a.m.
3. **I am a successful businessman.** As a publisher and connector, my role is to grow other people's businesses.

With those three intentions as part of my personal vision, when I wake up, is it hard to do what needs doing? Some days, it takes a lot of effort, but a king serves his community. There's no if or but or "feel like it" in that statement. An athlete trains his body. I can't press the snooze button. And my business? I thrive when I work on this.

Willpower is nowhere to be found in the above equation. I don't use it *except* when I want to push past a challenge to my goals; for instance, if I want to get faster at running the mile, or if I want to call five people for sales calls instead of three. That's the place for willpower. It's not to resist temptation, because if your intentions are set, you don't have to worry about temptation.

## Your Vision of You

Most of us don't have the first clue about our personal vision. We don't see ourselves beyond a very weakly defined definition. Who is easier to sway? Someone who doesn't really have a sense of herself, or someone who knows exactly what she wants from this planet?

Is it hard to build a vision of yourself? Not really. There are three parts to think about:

1. Where you *really* are now.
2. Where you want to be.
3. The keys to getting there.

That's not easy, but it's simple. We've said that before, but now you see it clearly, right?

Where you really are now—this is probably the hardest part, because we lie to ourselves on the one hand, and we treat ourselves very poorly on the other. For instance, when my coach wanted me to do a strength test, I wanted to complete five chin-ups. I got what I counted as four. He only gave me two (because the other two were crap). Where am I really? Two chin-ups. (Or was. I'm better now.)

Where you want to be is something you need to be very clear about. Not "successful." That's not where you want to be. You want to earn $1 million in annual revenue and be debt free with a home overlooking the downtown (or whatever your version of success is). You want to be "ready to sell my business in three years, with at least $10 million in payout," for example. Remember that these goals can be smaller: I could do two chin-ups. I want to do 10.

The keys to getting there can be found when you consider what the *daily* version of reaching your goals looks like. If you want $1 million a year, what are you going to do to get it? What's the process? Hint: This is probably the most important one of the three, but you have to know the first two to get this one.

Since implementing a daily practice to execute on my vision, it has removed my need for willpower for the day-to-day work of life, and it has given me a much better grasp of how I will accomplish my goals and receive the results I want. Can you exist without doing this? Certainly you can, but then how will you inherit the earth?

## Own the Mantle of Servant

Throughout this book, we've talked about serving a community being the key to business. Your *monchu* (the extended network you nurture) plus the community around the marketplace your work serves are the important parts of the puzzle. Where most people fail in business, it seems to me, is in forgetting this relationship.

You need only watch pop stars repeatedly shift from doing it "all for the fans" to "you should realize the privilege of loving my work." (By the way, I *loathe* the word "fan.")

We exist to serve our community. That's the most important mind-set to maintain. In this one detail, you can do the work you want to do and build the business you want to build, provided you've done the work we talked about before to identify the right community to serve.

The better you can manage that role, the more you commit to it, the more you can own everything.

For example: As I was writing this, a man wrote me back to tell me that he's enjoying his newsletter. He mentioned that he's building a website for his future plans right now. I replied to his note to ask him what he's doing going forward (I have zero business intentions behind this question; I'm being polite to someone who gives me his time by reading my newsletter). He replied, "I'm going to find an agent and publisher for a children's book project I have."

I immediately give him the means to connect to Katie Davis, the first person who comes to mind in my community who is a successful children's book author and book marketer. I give him ideas for his approach, let him use my name, and send him on his way to circumvent the painful learning process of not knowing anyone in the industry he intends to work in. Again, there's zero dollar value or business for me in this transaction.

But what I do get is the ability to deliver information to this man, who will now see me as someone eager to be helpful. I gave Katie Davis a chance to be the star she is (sometimes people don't know the stars they need to know), and I reinforce the very message I'm sharing with you, which is part of my personal vision of professional success.

This is how things get done. It's not your own capabilities. It's your capabilities and your network. But networks can be very cold. So instead, commit to the mantle of being a servant to a community and serve them as often as possible. It *will* improve your business and your future and your life.

Especially if you're a freak. Get to know the other freaks. If you are someone who paints sneakers to resemble My Little Pony characters, but you're not connected to the community of MLP fans, you're neglecting the people who will actually appreciate you. Connecting with them is a huge way to own your world.

## Own Your Freaky Self

I can't stress this enough: You can be just like everyone else and get what you can out of life or you can be a freak and inherit the earth. While I was typing this part, I was listening to the 2013 rewind from DJ Earworm (http://hbway.com/2013rewind). I actually played 2010, 2011, 2012, and 2013. What I was thinking the whole time was this: Only the freaks become big enough for us to notice.

And yet, so many of us up-and-coming freaks, so many of us freaks who haven't found our tribe yet, feel so wrong and so unlike everyone else who we encounter that we throw it all away. We hide. We sneak back under the veil of mediocrity. We're torn down, or worse, we surrender without a fight.

Being different is the hardest thing to own sometimes. There is no shortage of people who will want to take swings at you. There's no map for what to do next if you don't do what everyone else does. It's like nothing seems to fit.

But the best of everything in the world has come from freaks. All of it, I swear. Who first decided that taking some beans off a tree and roasting them for a bit, and throwing it all in hot water was a good idea? Coffee is delicious, but a freak created it. Every song you've ever sang over and over again was written by a freak. Every movie you love had freaks in it. All the most colorful things in life came from freaks.

Freaks in huge companies? Walt Disney was a freak. Sam Walton was a freak. Sir Richard Branson is a freak.

And before you go e-mailing me angrily that I named only male freaks, there's the real challenge I lay at your feet, my female freaks: The challenges to being a female freak in a huge company are so vast that we've rarely (if ever?) seen a woman achieve it. Marissa Mayer at Yahoo! can't afford to be a freak, because she has to be an amazing female CEO. (Totally unfair, you understand. But that's the pressure on female freaks.) Pepsico's Indra Nooyi? She's close, but still, she has to live up to conventional perceptions.

I would love to see the first amazing female freak being her own weird self at a huge corporation in my lifetime. Maybe that will be you. I hope with all my heart and soul that it is.

## Own Business

Business doesn't just magically happen, at least not all the time. You've got to make it happen. You've got to learn to be a better salesperson. You've got to learn to be a marketer. You've got to understand finances. You have a lot that will go into owning it.

Business is a daily part of your freak self, even if it's not what you envisioned for yourself. Business is just the world of exchanges, of commerce, of moving value back and forth between goods and services and currency. This is what feeds the rest of what you do. Very precious few humans can survive without transacting any kind of business, and usually, that's because they're at the mercy and in the care of others who do business to support them.

Own it. Own your business. It's not bad or evil or wrong to be in business, provided your intentions themselves aren't bad or evil or wrong. I'm a publisher and I sell courses and other products and services to people. I do this because I can add value to their lives.

Because of the value I add, I can extract some monetary value, which allows me to feed my kids and donate to causes and create occasional magic for people when they least expect it. I love business, because it's another kind of art.

And that's a daily commitment. You have to own it. Choose it. Be it. Thrive in it. That's where ownership comes in.

And how do we own anything? Invest in it daily. So what will you do daily to own your business? That's the challenge before us both.

## Own Your Future

The future is a weird thing. It's already here, only we haven't experienced it yet. And when I say that, let me get really practical and real about what I mean: If I eat a candy bar today, my belly will display that in a few days. If I stay in bed today, my bank will display that in a few days, too. The future is what I create today. Every day.

If you want to learn how to play the guitar, do you set a date three months from now and then just go about your days waiting for that day to come because then you will learn to play? No. You practice and learn. Every day. The more you practice, the more you learn. The more you mess up, the more you learn.

Your future is today. What you do today is how you own tomorrow. What am I doing today? Well, at the moment, I'm writing this book for you, which will help me with tomorrow (and hopefully for the next few years, if you end up telling others how much you like the book).

And remember when we talked about willpower? Owning your future is about having the discipline to execute your personal vision. That's where it all gets done.

But further, owning the future means investing in that community I refuse to stop talking about. The investments you make there daily become your future. That's what I've come to learn. Everything great in my life comes from my investment in other people whom I've come to know over time.

Every great thing that has happened in my life starting back years ago when I took an active interest in being the me I wanted to be came from growing that community around me, and that came from supporting them in their endeavors. That's the magic to your future. I promise.

We have one more chapter before the end of the main portion of this book. Here's where we talk about where it all might go wrong. Though it's a tough bit of work to deal with, I think it's important to include with everything else. You ready?

# 15  When It All Goes Wrong

Talk about a bummer chapter! We've been looking forward to the future and sharing some great thoughts and ideas on how to build your business your way, and now I've got to go and ruin it by talking about all the poopy things that can happen. There's a reason for this: A lot of times, this is what you'll really want to know about in a pinch. Heck, this might become your favorite chapter in the book (I hope not, but you never know).

Because things will go wrong. What? I don't know. Something will.

Maybe you'll build your entire business on top of someone else's technology and that base technology will shut down (that happened to me). Maybe you'll find that the marketplace that was working so well for one version of your business doesn't work for others for some reason and that you can't replicate your success in some way (that happened to me). Maybe you'll upset your business partner, run out of rent money, or some other great icky bad thing will happen. What then?

## Freaks Adapt

What you *don't* do is surrender. You might retreat occasionally, but you don't give up. You look for a way to make something else happen. Maybe the idea isn't too far from your original idea, but needs a tweak.

Perhaps a new approach is in order. Above all else, the mind-set is to accept that what you're doing is not working, and then figure out why. A quick framework may help you develop a new view.

## When Something Isn't Working

- Define what isn't working (money, people, resources, etc.).
- Is there a patch that will solve the problem (borrow money, find different people, locate new resources)?
- Do you have to abandon the goal as it is right now?
- How do you approach that?
- Take an action.
- Make the appropriate apologies.

This might not fit every single situation you'll run into, but it's a decent starting point for thinking through whatever might go wrong for you. Let's work through an example.

Maybe you decided you're in the "fantasy art character" business, where you paint lavish oil portraits of people's World of Warcraft characters, but you realize that your original price point of $50 for something that takes you 200 hours minimum might not be a really great price (I think that means you charged 25 cents an hour for your work, not counting materials).

First, list what you know to be the facts.

- You can't keep offering this.
- You'll have to decide what to do about people who have ordered and paid.

Let's use our little worksheet:

- Define what isn't working: The price is far too low for the effort involved.
- Is there a patch? Charge more or change the offering (like pencil art instead of oil painting).

- Do you have to abandon the goal as it is right now? Seems that way.
- How do you approach that? Figure out the customers' work you should *really* finish and do those, and offer refunds for the rest.
- Take an action. Follow through on what you just decided to do.
- Make the appropriate apologies. Apologize a lot and often.

What we haven't covered is "Now what?"

Let's go through what kinds of real-life situations will occur that will cause you to rethink what you're doing.

## What Do You Do the Day after You Realize You Have Problems?

First, we have to know what the problem is.

- Not enough money? You need to make more money, cut expenses, and figure out how to eat/sleep/survive.
- Owe someone money? Communication. You have to work out a plan to pay the person back, however that is going to happen.
- Need to rework the plan but need to do the previous steps at the same time? This happens often. You have to find temporary safety of some kind—maybe a "job."
- Did your team blow up in some way? Don't forget that if you have partners in your business, you have the potential for everything to break. I knew someone who had a business where she was the creative and her partner was the salesperson. When things got too quiet and money just wasn't coming in, the salesperson quit, leaving the creative person with no way to drum up business herself (at least not immediately).

Once you have challenges, you have to solve them in a kind of Maslow's Hierarchy of Needs sort of way (Google that, if need be).

- **Food and shelter.** Do you and/or whoever depends on you have enough money to eat and have a place to stay? This is priority number one. If it means getting a job, selling your impressive Super Nintendo cartridge collection on eBay, or whatever else, you need to keep yourself and others alive.

- **Start of debt management.** If you're way underwater in debt, you at least have to figure out a way to get a trickle of money started back to pay off those debts while you work on fixing everything else. Even if it's $5 a month (pretty weak, but you never know), that's better than nothing. And you owe people a lot of communication. We all want to clam up when we're broke, but that never helps.
- **Find money.** Early on, once things crash and burn, you've got to earn some loot. Maybe you sell things. Maybe you take two jobs. Maybe you ask around for loans. But you almost never get out of the hole of your business crashing without money, and so you've got to make that happen. (And yet, working *solely* for money sounds as desperate as it is, so tread gently.)
- **Build a new starter plan.** It's *so* important that your new plan not be "And now I will create a rival to Walmart" or "now, my band and I will go on tour and blow Lada Gaga's concert revenues away." The plan should be more like: "If I can sell $500 a week of my services and a few products, then I can feel more comfortable about covering my rent/mortgage/car payment."
- **Build the bigger plan.** The bigger plan is getting you back in the freak business. Hint: It can't look like the last plan all that much. That plan didn't work. Remember?
- **Massive debt repayment.** Get your trickle up to something better and start living in the black.

So that's the goal ladder:

- Secure food/shelter.
- Start any debt repayment trickle.
- Find money.
- Build the new starter plan.

- Build the bigger plan.
- Massive debt repayment (if any).

What do you think? Make sense for you?

# Apologizing

Oh, if only I could teach the universe how to be better at apologizing, I think the universe would be a much better place. One of the things we humans do somewhat worse than most other things is to say "sorry" in a useful and meaningful way. I've got a little bit of advice on this, because it turns out that if you ever try to do something that's beyond the norm—you know, freak stuff—you will mess up somewhere, and you will have to apologize. Ready?

## The Three A's

I first mentioned the Three A's in Chapter 5. I learned about this concept a million years ago while training to be a waiter in a restaurant (I was very bad at this job, by the way). The concept is simple. The "best way" to apologize, according to the trainer, was to Acknowledge, Apologize, Act. In the restaurant world, for example, an owner might interact with a customer in the following way.

- **Acknowledge.** Your food isn't ready to be served yet. It really has been a long time.
- **Apologize.** I'm really sorry for the delay.
- **Act.** I'm going to credit you for your appetizer and may I give you your next drink on the house?

There—it's that simple. Note what I didn't do: make excuses, accept blame (which is very different from apologizing), or say nothing and hope that no one noticed what was wrong.

There are so many ways to do this worse.

## "But" Apologies

"I'm really sorry I hit you in the head with that bat, Ricky, *but* you snuck up on me and scared me." The "but" eliminates the validity of the apology, right? Another example might be "I'm sorry I kissed your girlfriend, *but* she was hot."

## Blame Shifting

"I'm really sorry I didn't deliver that Assassin's Creed fan art I promised you, but Kevin never brought back my drawing tablet, so I had to wait a wicked long time and . . ." And no one cares, and they are still frustrated that you didn't take responsibility for the delay.

## Checklist for Effective Apologies

Here's a quick checklist:

* Acknowledge that whatever happened, happened.
* Apologize in simple and clear fashion, using the words "I'm sorry."
* Act in a way that will help the situation and/or prevent it from happening again in the future.
* Do *not* qualify the apology with any "but" language. (Don't be a "but"-head.)
* Do *not* shift blame to anyone else. You're apologizing because you have a responsibility and/or a relationship with the person you're talking with, and that's what matters. It doesn't matter whether or not you're at fault; handle the problems on your own. Your customer isn't required to weigh in on who is to blame.

Good? Great. These are the important points when apologizing. Will you have to apologize in your business career? Yes. No question about it. Especially if you're daring to do something interesting and new.

## Thoughts on Failure

As I first mentioned in Chapter 3, Anthony Robbins said that the best way we can view failure is to think of things that go wrong as "outcomes we didn't want or expect." This one piece of advice can be very powerful. You were hoping to sell 200 of your handcrafted beeswax candles, and you sold 20. Are you a failure? No. You simply didn't achieve the outcome that you desired.

When you free yourself from the guilt and other negativity that we assign to the idea of "failure," you find yourself open to come up with more ways to achieve the outcomes that you want, or to have a new perspective on outcomes that might be even better. It's a huge relief, this mind-set. Instead of failing, you've found a different outcome. Will that work for you?

It's up to you to practice. This mind-set doesn't come naturally. And if you're the only one practicing it, others will still call you a failure when things don't turn out the way you want. But this is not your problem to deal with. If you accept this concept, you simply have to work on getting the outcomes you want.

Here's a personal experience: I've always wanted to write fiction, ever since I was a young boy (maybe five years old). I still haven't written a fiction book. But I've published seven books (so far) and now I am a *New York Times* best-selling author (as well as being on best-seller lists in *Inc.,* the *Wall Street Journal, USA Today,* and *800-CEO-Read*). Does that make me a failure? Heck no.

## Depression and Other Excuses

Lots of people who are creative and unique and freaks like you and me are also the type of people who can become depressed. Some of you might even have depression that makes it really, really hard to get out of bed. Or maybe you have seasonal affective disorder. You probably have many excuses why you can't succeed or win.

Adopt a "yes, and" approach to your depression or other excuses.

Maybe you were abused as a child. Yes, and you owe it to yourself to be the freak you want to be and find success.

Maybe your spouse just left you. Yes, and now it's time to be the *you* that you've always wanted to be.

Maybe your business partner took all the money and ran off. Yes, and now you have to do something next.

It's not okay to allow anything to be used as an excuse. Excuses are just a tool of settling, and we don't believe in settling. You might surrender sometimes, but you never settle. It's not okay to quit (at least not forever). It's not okay to go back to bed and be depressed instead of doing what needs to be done.

Yes, you are flawed in some way and broken and otherwise impaired or hampered, *and* it's still your duty to inherit the earth.

## Actions and Next Steps

Okay, we have one last chapter, which is the action chapter. Admittedly, there are recommended actions throughout this book, but the last chapter is even more focused on actions to take to achieve your goals. We just survived the bummer chapter; now let's go to the "Okay, time to fight crime!" chapter.

# 16 Take Action! Fight Crime! Save the World!

This entire book is worthless, if you don't take action. If you've read anything before and thought, "Yeah, that really made me feel good" and then went back to whatever it is you're doing, you'll know what I mean. This first became obvious to me when I started tracking how people talked about my books online. Here's what I'd see, over and over again:

> Just finished *Trust Agents*. Now on to read *The New Rules of Marketing and PR*.

People seem to believe that finishing a book is the same as doing something with the information. You, friend, have the opportunity to leap past your well-read friends who opted not to take any specific actions. Yes, you have the chance to take action, fight crime, and save the world!

## Step 1: Declare Your Freakiness (Even If Only to Yourself)

First off, admit that you're a freak, and by that I mean that you intend to do business your way, that you want business to be personal, that you believe that the best business is the kind that keeps your heart in mind along the way. In fact, jump on Twitter and tweet me: @chrisbrogan and use the hashtag #proudfreak. Say hi! I'll talk back!

## Step 2: Define Your Own Success

How will you know you're doing well if you have no idea what success means to you? You have to list out, literally on paper or in your favorite note-taking software, a definition of success. It has to be really specific:

- 1,000 regular customers.
- $1 million a year in revenue.
- Running an eight-minute mile.

Whatever makes your success yours, list it out. Try to list a success criteria for each role that's important in your life and for your success.

## Step 3: Learn Some New Skills

You know your strengths. Start working on your weaknesses. Commit to learning one new skill every two or three months. Study marketing, sales, basic finance, and more. Commit to this. Put it in your schedule. This is an area where most people fall down, and if you take an action, you can succeed.

## Step 4: Work from a Framework Daily

I'm writing this right now because my schedule and framework say that it's what needs to be done. What I'd rather be doing is reading a magazine I just bought. But working from a framework is how you will succeed. You'll do more. You'll build discipline. Life will be much more magical.

## Step 5: Define Your Path

You might be an employeepreneur, happily working for The Man. You might be looking to leap into a solo gig, or to run your own business empire. But know where you are, know what matters to where you are at this moment, and know where you're going next. If you don't write down your path and your destination, how will you know where you want to go?

## Step 6: Fall in Love with Not Knowing

This is such a powerful opportunity for you: Learn to be okay with the unknown, and learn how to really appreciate what comes next in the universe. Practice the battle plan for failure in this book, and learn how to thrive.

## Step 7: Worship Obstacles and Challenges

One way to face obstacles is to set a new challenge for yourself every month. For instance, I have a list that I call the "face this" list. It's a list of all the various challenges I normally shy away from. It's an interesting list. For instance, I have "Call Frank from the IRS" on my list. The more challenges I face daily, the stronger I feel about doing more with my business and my life. It's a good list to have.

## Step 8: Create Systems That Work for You

Similar to the framework step, you've got to take action to build systems that work for you. For instance, I just implemented a system that lays out every half hour of my waking day so that I can put the "stuff" that needs doing into "blocks." I have to place at least one kind of block each day, because the blocks represent those kinds of tasks I decided are important to the success of my business. A principle I'm setting for myself is "No meetings for more than 20 minutes" and another is "No phone meetings when e-mail will solve the issue." Make systems and stick to them, at least for a month or two.

## Step 9: Build Your Media Empire

This is a step you might be eager to skip. Making media of any kind isn't everyone's bag. But this is where the most benefit will come to you. Start wherever you can: a blog, or photos on Instagram/Pinterest, or YouTube, and build your world up a little at a time. This is the big benefit others won't likely copy and it's where you can get ahead.

## Step 10: Connect with Your Freaks

Make this promise with yourself: "I will connect with three new people a day, five if I want to be amazing." The more you can find the people you seek to serve, the better your opportunities. Connect with people you can help. Connect two people who might benefit from knowing each other. Do everything you can to keep your network (your *monchu*!) alive and well.

## Step 11: Own Everything

The more you can take ownership the better. Start with owning your words. Keep a list of words not to say, and make a new list of words that empower your ownership. From there, work on owning your choices. Commit to making positive choices in your life, and see how much you can grow in any given month.

## Step 12: Be Ready for the Bad Times

Remember that you can hit bumps in the road at any time. Be ready. Know how to apologize (the Three A's described in Chapter 15). Be ready to assess what needs doing when there are issues. Know whether or not you have to pull the plug. And keep your mind open to how your ideas might have to shift.

## Take Action. Any Action

The biggest difference between you and others who will just accept what life and work brings them is that you've chosen to take action. The big opportunity for you is to do something based on ideas that came while reading this book, and through the rest of your experiences.

Where do you start? Anywhere. That's the deal. It's better to start somewhere than wait around for the chance of doing everything in order. Obstacles are just an opportunity to get you to start something new, or work on another task.

This is your moment. Draw up your plans, simple ones, and go after them. Take your shot. And if it doesn't work, take another, and another, and win.

See? This is the method, the mind-set, and the way. Or it's one way, a way that has served other misfits and freaks and nonstandard humans who have gone on to live life and do business on their own terms. Are you ready to join them?

One last note: If ever you want to reach me, drop me an e-mail: chris@ownermag.com. I'm always happy to talk with people who have questions or who want to take action on what they have learned in this book.

Go freaks! (Remember to use the hashtag #proudfreak to connect with others like you!)

# Index